Hollywood Beyond
the Screen

MATERIALIZING CULTURE
. . . .

Series Editors: Paul Gilroy, Michael Herzfeld and Danny Miller

Barbara Bender, *Stonehenge: Making Space*

Gen Doy, *Materializing Art History*

Laura Rival (ed.), *The Social Life of Trees: Anthropological Perspectives on Tree Symbolism*

Victor Buchli, *An Archaeology of Socialism*

Marius Kwint, Christopher Breward and Jeremy Aynsley (eds), *Material Memories: Design and Evocation*

Penny Van Esterik, *Materializing Thailand*

Michael Bull, *Sounding Out the City: Personal Stereos and the Management of Everyday Life*

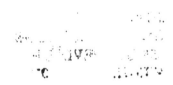

Hollywood Beyond the Screen

Design and Material Culture

ANNE MASSEY

Oxford • New York

First published in 2000 by
Berg
Editorial offices:
150 Cowley Road, Oxford, OX4 1JJ, UK
838 Broadway, Third Floor, New York, NY 10003-4812, USA

Berg is the imprint of Oxford International Publishers Ltd.

Library of Congress Cataloging-in-Publication Data

A catalogue record for this book is available from the Library of
Congress.

British Library Cataloguing-in-Publication Data

A catalogue record for this book is available from the British Library.

ISBN 1 85973 316 6 (Cloth)
      1 85973 321 2 (Paper)

Typeset by JS Typesetting, Wellingborough, Northants.
Printed in the United Kingdom by Biddles Ltd, Guildford and
King's Lynn.

Contents

List of Figures

Acknowledgements

My thanks to Dr Judy Attfield, Mike Hammond, Professor Pat Kirkham, Dr Wendy Leeks, Dr Esther Sonnet and Pete Stanfield for invaluable help and information in putting the book together. To Emma Stoffer, who acted as a model research assistant for the book. Thanks are also due to the staff of Southampton Institute and the Media Arts Faculty, who supported a sabbatical for me to write up the research; special thanks to Humphry Trevelyan for performing brilliantly as Acting Dean. Thanks to Dr Marius Kwint who suggested to Berg Publishers I write the book and to Kathryn Earle for commissioning it. Thanks also to the National Monuments Record Office, Swindon, the Hartley Library, University of Southampton, the RIBA Library, Bournemouth Public Library, Poole Public Library, the Cornwall Studies Library, the 20th Century Society, the Sydney Jones Library, University of Liverpool, *Country Life*, Penlee House Gallery and Museum, the British Film Institute, Dr Annette Kuhn, Dr Upton, Steve Thomas, Farbo Nairn Floor Covering and David Thacker of the Butlin's Archive.

Special thanks to my family for sharing their memories and responses to Hollywood with me. This book is dedicated to my grandmother, Sarah Carr, who inspired my initial love of history and fascination with Hollywood.

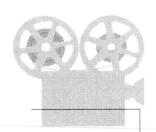

Introduction: Reclaiming the Personal and the Popular

This book is about tying up loose ends. It offers a reading of visual culture that makes new links between design and film, using an approach taken from material culture studies. It also offers insights into the Americanization of British popular culture by looking at changing representations and meanings of glamour. The book also ties up some loose ends in my own personal history. I began writing it at a moment of alienation; its inspiration came from an urge to prove just what an 'outsider' I was, contrasted with all the perceived 'insiders' who surrounded me. I wanted to prove that my north-eastern English, working-class background was a major handicap and source of not belonging in the academy. I felt like an alien northerner working in the comfortable and prosperous south of England. The loose ends were going to remain exactly that – their virtue was in their marginality from the main fabric of academic debate.

However, having now worked through the project over the past two years I have reached a different understanding. Further research revealed to me just how many other white women who came from similar backgrounds to myself had made a major contribution to the under-standing of popular culture.[1] This changed perception was also informed by the writings of black women working in the academy and respect for their experience, for example the Distinguished Professor of English at City University of New York, bel hooks, who wrote: 'As a black woman intellectual working overtime to call attention to feminist thinking, to issues of sexism, one who wanted to talk about the convergence of race, sex, and class, I found films to be the perfect cultural texts' (1996: 5). The divisions of insider/outsider or core/periphery became more blurred as I looked closer. I came to realize that I was passing responsi-bility for my self-understanding and self-perception to others, whom I then hated for taking it. As Valerie Walkerdine has argued:

1

On one level, the idea that we are constructed in the male gaze is reassuring. We remain somehow not responsible for our actions, as thought we were mere puppets to masculinity. . . . It strikes me as easier to take apart a beautiful image, blame patriarchy, and yet hold on to that image (Yes, yes, I am that really) or to point to a void as its other side than to examine what else may lurk there beneath (1991: 36).

Therefore, I have reclaimed an understanding of and responsibility for my self and my inheritance, the popular and glamorous that has formed a part of me. I offer it in (I believe) a generous and positive spirit. I hope that the understanding I bring to the subject of links between Hollywood and design, informed by my own experiences, my family history, local history, research into contemporary sources plus other academics' significant work on the subject, will prove useful as an interdisciplinary study. I see it as entirely central to the growing academic project of studying the personal and the popular, and I want to be there in the centre of it. Chris Weedon has argued:

For women active in the literary and educational institutions the task of transformation may seem overwhelming. It is important that we continue to be involved in and maintain supportive strategic links with the wider feminist movement, claiming and using the institutional power available to us but always with a view to subverting it and making resistant discourses and subject positions much more widely available (1997: 169).

This book argues that popular Hollywood film has had a major impact on the material culture of Britain from at least the 1920s until the present day. A direct link is made between the transient, two-dimensional image projected on the screen and the more permanent, three-dimensional artefact. This link to Hollywood manifested itself in all areas of design and consumption – from buildings, interiors, advertising to clothing and beauty products, as well as theories of design. A new type of building – the cinema – was created to enable the public to see films *en masse,* and new types of glamour were portrayed for the first time on film and made available to women through the mass production techniques of the age of modernity. Patterns of speech, ways of smoking a particular brand of cigarette or embracing a partner were acted out on the screen and emulated. This book aims to correlate important trends in design with changes within classical Hollywood cinema and seek explanations for these links in terms of economic, social and political forces. The book adopts the structure established by film historians to label the different stages in terms of technology, production and reception. Therefore, the first chapter explores film and design from the end of the First World War until the Wall Street crash – a period that Gaylyn Studlar has termed the 'Jazz Age' (1996: 1). Chapter 2 then examines the first decade of Classical Hollywood cinema, when sound was introduced and glamour was represented by a *moderne* style rather than earlier art deco, with a particular focus on the local and the global context through an investigation of design on the south coast of England (Bordwell, Staiger and Thompson: 1988). Chapter 3 looks at the cinema during and just after the Second World War, the second stage of Classical Hollywood cinema. The final chapter examines Post-Classical Hollywood in relation to post-modernism and a fragmented consumer culture. Each chapter examines, in turn, film history in America and Britain; the arrival of and reactions to Hollywood film in Britain; and then associated trends in architecture and design.

The four chapters mesh with the four generations of my own family – from my two grandmothers, who copied selected Hollywood stars in their clothes, make-up and hairstyles; my mother and father, who were impressed and influenced by Hollywood fashion, hairstyles and behaviour as depicted on film; myself, deeply affected by the lifestyle and motor-cycles depicted in *Easy Rider* (1969) and the glamour of Julia Roberts in the transformational Cinderella tale *Pretty Woman* (1990), through to my daughters, obsessed with the new *Titanic* (1998). Being fans of Hollywood film and how that fandom affects lives in some shape or form is the common element that links these four generations of my family, a lineage that I now realize I was trying to make some sense of at a time of personal crisis. The glamour of modernity spoke to me as a way of understanding the images and memories of these four generations and my own place within them. It offered a way of examining shared and individual experiences of modernity as alienated involvement, pleasure and unease, as belonging, dislocation, divorce and dis-ease.[2] It demanded an examination from the inside, necessarily intellectual, theoretical, historical, yet encompassing and recognizing the emotional and, perhaps above all, the subjective import of objects.

This study is interdisciplinary and cuts across different boundaries. It relates to and draws upon film studies, cultural studies, media studies, gender studies, local history, design history and the study of visual culture, but is not strictly speaking located within any one discourse. By considering the broader context of the moving image in terms of edifices and artefacts, a new perspective on the Americanization of British culture is offered from an object-based, material culture position tied particularly to the history of design. The book links avant-garde practice in design with popular, visual imagery. This introduction explores the material culture of film and seeks to explain its comparative lack of coverage to date. The main explanation lies in the discourse of academia itself, in its foundation upon certain common-sense assumptions about social class, gender, race and shared cultural values that have increasingly been open to challenge. There is a growing body of work that reflects on the practice of being an academic in terms of working either as a researcher, a manager or a teacher.[3] This introduction argues from my own position within academia, where affirmation of my own history and experience seems to be missing – that lack is addressed through the consideration of the material culture of film as a significant historical entity worthy of serious study. In demonstrating the legitimacy of examining the subjective import of objects as constitutive of the social, I assert the presence of my past and my self.

Material Culture and Design History

The new approach offered by material culture is key to unravelling the impact of film beyond the act of spectatorship and watching the film itself. Originating in nineteenth-century anthropology, the study of material culture offers an academic framework for analysing the material world. It was defined in 1875 by A. Lane-Fox Pitt-Rivers, founder of the Pitt-Rivers Museum in Oxford, as '. . . the outward signs and symbols of particular ideas in the mind' (as quoted by Schlereth 1990: 19). For the purposes of this book, material culture is defined as the study of how people have used objects to cope with and interpret their physical world.

The leading British academic in the field, Daniel Miller, has been central in the adoption of material culture studies beyond the discipline of anthropology. The publication of his *Material Culture and Mass Consumption* in 1987 marked a significant moment in the wider interest in the approach in Britain. The book appeared when the impact of post-modernism was prompting a re-evaluation by design historians of the intentionality and role of the designer and the credibility of the hegemony of the modern movement. Design history developed, in the 1970s, from the need to teach design students aspects of theory apart from traditional art history. As such, it tended to be designer- and object-focused rather than more broadly centred around ideas. The *Journal of Design History*, the leading academic publication in the field, concentrates largely on publishing detailed surveys of the work of designers, businesses or groups of objects. The strategy pursued by the subject's leading figures of building up a basis of empirical research resulted in a certain marginalization of design history as a discipline. The prevalence of 'good design' as a subject and worthy organizations, like the Design Council, as major foci has led to the neglect of everyday as opposed to avant-garde design. It has also led to a concentration on production as opposed to consumption.

My own starting-point in terms of design history was first of all studying the subject when it was in its infancy on the undergraduate programme at Newcastle Polytechnic in the late 1970s. From there I studied the work of the Independent Group for a Ph.D. at the same institution (Massey: 1995). This helped to address the relative lack of interest in the popular and the everyday in terms of visual culture. My first degree had given me a grounding in the new art history, and in the emerging discipline of film studies as well as critical theory. The work of the Independent Group, I now realize, gave me a way of studying how art, design and popular culture interrelate. The Group acknowledged the importance of the popular, and did not dismiss it as disinterested intellectuals, but sought to explain the allure of consumption as they had experienced it themselves. It was also important to me that the Group included important women theorists and practitioners and that all members of the Group acknowledged the importance of the female consumer. Apart from the work of the Independent Group, feminist design historians have succeeded in producing a broadranging account of popular taste that acknowledges the context in which design operates.

Pat Kirkham and Judy Attfield's introduction to *The Gendered Object* (1996) considered a broad sweep of design objects and defined design as: '. . . as material artefact, commodity, aesthetic object, *aide-memoire*, souvenir, lifestyle, political symbol; signifier supreme' (1996: 3). Combined with the approach of the sociologist Colin Campbell, it led into considerations of consumption and the consumer in a broader cultural context (1987, 1998). As Daniel Miller argued in *Acknowledging Consumption: A Review of New Studies*, the: '. . . study of consumption does not seem to represent merely an additional trajectory, what is striking in their juxtaposition within this volume is that the study of consumption seems to present a fundamental challenge to the basic premises that have sustained each discipline up to the present. That this should happen in a single discipline might call for little further comment, but that there seems to be emerging evidence for an "across the board" sea-change suggests something rather more fundamental with regard to the significance of consumption itself' (1995: 1). Whilst Miller has led the application of a material culture approach to many related academic areas in Britain beyond anthropology, the approach adopted in America differs in context and application.

The material culture approach was adopted beyond anthropology in America during the 1980s, in particular by curatorial staff at leading museums of American history including the Smithsonian Institution in Washington DC and the Winterthur Museum, Delaware. *History from Things: Essays on Material Culture* (ed. Lubar and Kingery), published in 1993 as a result of the international conference, 'History From Things: The Use of Objects in Understanding the Past' held at the Smithsonian in 1989, helped to make sense of the rich collection of the Smithsonian, which did not strictly adhere to late twentieth-century notions of academic respectability, museum categorization or aesthetic quality. It was rather an important index of the way people lived, of their values and of their culture in its broadest sense. At the time of writing, interpretative exhibits at the Smithsonian's National Museum of American History included *A Material World*, with a 1946 AMI Model A Jukebox and an aluminium sign dating from 1938 for the streamlined *20th Century Limited* train; an exhibit that charts the history of the clothes-peg; and the flag that inspired Francis Scott Key to write *The Star-Spangled Banner* in 1812. This is complemented by an exhibit that charts the migration of black Americans from the South to the industrial North in the early twentieth century, using reconstructions of rooms and a segregated train car, contemporary toys and documentary photographs. As Jules David Prown declared in *History From Things*: '. . . the study of material culture is the study of material to understand culture, to discover the beliefs – the values, ideas, attitudes, and assumptions – of a particular community or society at a given time' (ed. Lubar and Kingery 1993: 1). The aim of this book is to consider particular design styles as a way of understanding the lived culture of British society during the twentieth century.

The approach offered by material culture has informed design-historical studies, but it has not informed any work on the reception of film as such. Daniel Miller does discuss suburbia in *Material Culture and Mass Consumption*, and raises pertinent queries about the role of professional architects in the design of mass housing in a modern style whilst preferring to live in a traditional dwelling themselves. The architectural historian, Anthony King, touched on the key question of lack of coverage of ordinary culture in his book, *The Bungalow: The Production of a Global Culture*, suggesting: 'The most plausible explanation for what is apparently a conscious decision either to ignore or, if recognising, to disparage it [the bungalow], would seem to be in the class attitudes towards the bungalow developed in Britain between the wars and which have persisted since then' (King 1995: 4). The same could be said of the material culture of cinema. The quotation from King highlights an important aspect of looking at popular culture and of academic practice at large. In *Dunroamin : The Suburban Semi and Its Enemies,* the authors recount training as architects in the 1950s and feeling embarrassed by their humble origins in a semi-detached house in the northern fringe of London (Oliver, Davis and Bentley 1981).

The writing of Miller is important in offering an all-inclusive category for the history of objects. His work also offers an insight into the knowledge production industry itself and the work of the academic left:

> The argument that there is a thing called capitalist society which renders its population entirely pathological and dehumanized, with the exception of certain theorists who, although inevitably living their private lives in accordance with the tenets of this delusion, are able in their abstracted social theory to rise above, criticize and provide the only alternative model for society, is somewhat suspicious. The clear lesson from the history of modernism is that the academic left is quite capable of fashioning a central instrument for the reproduction of the interests of the dominant class at precisely the moment when it is making the most strident claims to the contrary (1987:167).

In answer to my question about the apparent neglect of the popular in academic writing, it should be noted that most established academics in the past were male, white and hailed from middle-class or even upper-class backgrounds. If they did come from 'other' backgrounds, they had to adopt or adapt to at least some of the assumptions of the academic world if they were to be accepted. This included the ruling ideology about being dismissive of popular culture and of consumption. Notable exceptions in the development of British cultural studies include the work of Raymond Williams and, in history, E. P. Thompson (Williams 1958; Thompson 1963). One need only consider the disparaging coverage of the disciplines of Media and Cultural Studies not only, in the 'quality' British broadsheets like *The Independent* and *The Guardian,* but even in the *Times Higher Education Supplement,* where they form the subject of a weekly satirical column by Laurie Taylor, right up until the present day. Fashion and costume for the screen are still frowned upon as frivolous by some,[4] and there is a shared, unspoken assumption that all American popular culture is trash that is perceived as a threat to authentic British cultural life, most evidently in the British press (Massey and Hammond 1999). This is underscored by the discourse of linking the popular with the feminine and obsolescent and 'high culture' with the masculine and everlasting (Modleski 1986; Huyssen 1986). And it is further reflected in the gender bias in academic life, whereby the higher one goes, the fewer women there are in post. For example, only 8 per cent of professors in Britain are women; and as one of those women I want to help establish a serious study of the popular that challenges these divisions.[5]

As Daniel Miller has noted: 'It is argued that these global approaches almost always move from an attack on contemporary material culture as trivial or inauthentic to an implied (though rarely explicit) denigration of the mass of the population whose culture this is' (Miller 1987: 16). Some post-modern writers have been similarly dismissive of contemporary, popular experiences. The French philosopher Jean Baudrillard bemoaned the end of the society of the spectacle in 1983 and its replacement with the age of simulacrum, where nothing is real and everything a copy. As Nicholas Mirzoeff observed in *Visual Culture*: '. . . Baudrillard's nostalgia for a past in which a "basic reality" could actually be experienced is analogous to the American critic Frederick Jameson's Marxist critique of what he sees as the image culture of "late capitalism"' (1999: 28). However, the situation is more complex than this. The post-modern project has also enabled a reconsideration of the popular and a rediscovery of past writers who have valorized mass culture, for example, the work of the German critic, Walter Benjamin. His writing and research during the inter-war years in Paris have attracted the attention of important cultural studies critics, particularly his unfinished *Passagenwerk* project, in which he examined the subtle attractions of an aspirational consumer culture (McRobbie: 1994: 96–120).

There is thankfully a growing acceptance of the study of the popular in academic circles, fuelled by a new generation of academics working on projects in a diverse range of disciplines. For example, Media Studies has now entered the curriculum of courses at the London School of Economics and Cultural Studies at Oxford University. An important moment in the acceptance of the popular was the staging, in 1981, of the British Open University's U203 course, *Popular Culture,* on which I was privileged to teach. This drew upon the tradition of the Centre for Contemporary Cultural Studies at Birmingham University, whose first director, Richard Hoggart, published *The Uses of Literacy* in 1958.[6]

Teaching on the *Popular Culture* summer school in 1982 I was struck by one project that illustrates my unease with Cultural Studies at that point. This consisted of a trip to the seaside resort of Blackpool, on which students were charged with bringing back the most tacky souvenir they could find. This caused great hilarity as students boarded the coaches for their trip, many wearing 'weeny boppers' on their head.[7] I was uncomfortable with this experience, as my paternal grandmother was a regular visitor to Blackpool, particularly during the autumn on a much-treasured day trip to view the illuminations, a specially themed display of lights that decorates the main promenade each year. It felt as if middle-class academics were poking fun at working-class experiences. The course itself tended to seek out oppositional readings of popular culture, informed by the writing of Antonio Gramsci, Althusser and Dick Hebdige. We heard rap poetry about 'there ain't no black in the union jack' and studied reworkings of Constable's Haywain to publicize the CND. But we still laughed at souvenirs.

The fascination with oppositional readings has underscored much subsequent work on popular culture. This at once alienates the experience of the majority and marginalizes the academic project itself. Dominic Strinati and Stephen Wagg, writing in their introduction to *Come on Down? Popular Media Culture in Post-War Britain* still treasure the marginality of the study of the popular and its political project (1992: 3). As Mirzoeff has argued when discussing the death of Princess Diana:

> Popular culture has been received into the academy on the basis that it 'really' allows people to address serious issues behind the surface vulgarity. Diana's death forces us to realize that the distinction is, like all such distinctions, a form of elitism that wants to separate the serious wheat of popular experience from the chaff of its vulgarity. For the subcultures so celebrated in the cultural studies writings of the 1980s have given way first to fan cultures like those of science fiction and now to the mediatized world of post-fandom. (Redhead 1997) The British Left, from which cultural studies originated, was so badly wrong about the Diana phenomenon precisely because of its profound distrust of images and appearance' (1999: 233).

Whilst it is true that the early work of cultural studies, film studies and design history took place on the margins, and there was difficulty in getting accepted, it is now time to place the study of the popular and the personal into the centre.

Family History

Like those of many historians who have popularized the study of popular culture, my geographic and social origins and gender are still not common amongst university professors. My own academic interest in the popular is not informed by distance, by looking at a strange, foreign activity, but by feeling inside and part of the process of consumption. My paternal grandfather, Harry Massey, was born in 1909 and came from an army background; he served as a Sergeant-Major until 1947. He then worked at the Consett Iron Company, or *The Works* as it is known locally, as a gas engineer until early retirement through ill health in 1971. He died prematurely of gangrene in 1975, caused initially by a foot injury sustained in a fall in a fish and chip shop in Bridlington. The gangrene was worsened by his heavy smoking of the high tar cigarettes – Capstan Full Strength – advertised during the Second World War as good for the nerves and his working conditions. There is currently an investigation under way into the high incidence of cancer amongst those who were employed at *The Works*. The red dust that covered the town from 1964, when oxygen steel-making was introduced, is thought to have had an impact on health. I can recall the thick, red dust lying on the pure white Durham snow as we drove as a family to Consett for Christmas visits, plus the pungent smell of gas. This certainly did not resemble the purity of the snow I had experienced in Walt Disney's *Bambi* (1942) at the age of six. As Alex Watson, leader of Derwentside District Council, recently recalled: 'The red dust belched out, clouds of it, and it rained dust in Consett – everybody got covered in muck. Windows, trees, roads, the entire infrastructure corroded and crumbled' (Hadley 1998: 31). My mother, who also grew up in the area and loved to wear fashionable clothes, recalls standing at a bus stop in a new beige coat and being covered in red dust.

My paternal grandmother, Violet Green, was born in 1913 and proved to be a bright pupil, attending High Westwood School, a 'cut above' that in Consett. However, she left to work for the local Italian ice-cream shop owners when she was 14 in 1927, the year after the breaking of the General Strike brought worsening conditions to the mining areas of the North-East of England. She then went to Hampshire to work as a maid in a large, turn-of-the-century red-brick house set in its own grounds, Wenham Holt near Liss. The family she worked for had show business connections, and living in Hampshire enabled her and her cousin, who also worked in the house, to travel to London to see West

End shows. This included *Showboat*, starring the black American star Paul Robeson.[8] Dressed as glamorously as her means would allow (she was an enthusiastic and able home dressmaker) she met my grandfather in 1932 at a local dance whilst he was stationed at an army camp in Surrey. Like many women from the North, she travelled south to earn money to send back home during the economic depression of 1929–1931. After marrying, the couple had their first child, who was named Harry after his father and is my father, in 1933; but the second son (born in 1934) was named after the film star Raymond Massey. My grandfather had to leave the army, as he could not support his family on a single man's pay – married pay only started from the age of 25. He worked for a time as a builder's labourer, helping to construct extensions to the London Underground. When that work ran out my grandparents moved back to Consett and lived with my grandmother's parents in their two-bedroomed miner's cottage. My grandfather eventually found a job at *The Works*, which thankfully also provided a house. During all these years my grandmother, a huge fan of Hollywood cinema, would go to the pictures at least twice weekly and, in common with thousands of women of her age and class, model her clothes and hair-styles on those of Hollywood stars (Figure 1).

My maternal grandmother, Sarah Johnson, was born in 1911 and shared a similar enthusiasm for Hollywood – aiming to look like Clara Bow during the 1920s and convinced she looked like Olivia de Havilland in the 1930s (Figures 2 and 3). She passed the examination to attend grammar school, but her parents could not afford to let her go – instead she travelled to Manchester to be a housemaid. She then met my maternal grandfather, Tom Carr, one year her senior, who worked in the mining industry as a colliery blacksmith, looking after the pit ponies. He then worked for Vickers-Armstrong in their armaments factory on the river Tyne. However, an accident left his back permanently damaged. Whilst in hospital he passed the long hours drawing sketches of his favourite pastime – fox-hunting, which he had taken part in since he was a child.[9] After the war he was able to enter King's College School of Art in Newcastle upon Tyne on the strength of his artistic talent.[10] He was taught by the leading illustrative printmaker, Vernon Stokes, and subsequently pursued earning a living as an artist, unable to undertake heavy manual work or indeed ride horses after the accident.

The question of social class becomes blurred, as my grandfather's gift, which he used to paint and sketch horses, led to commissions from aristocratic patrons, beginning with the Duke of Northumberland

Figure 1 Violet Massey (*née* Green – my Grandmother) 1939

and then the Duke of Buccleuch. Memorable parts of my childhood were spent accompanying my grandfather to stately homes while he sketched horses or delivered paintings. But there was always a recogniz-able barrier there, when I was told in hushed tones not to talk and not to expect to be invited into the house. This was not really a 'place for us', we were there to offer the fruits of my grandfather's labour and nothing else.

My mother was born in 1935 and inherited my grandfather's artistic gifts, and trained as an art and physical education teacher, supporting my father to train as an architect during the 1950s. Their joint escape route from the struggles of growing up in the depression and the war, for my father from going down the mines and for my mother from shop work, was through education and developing creative talents. My mother went on to be a pioneering and award-winning education officer at the Laing Art Gallery in Newcastle upon Tyne, and my father founded his own successful architectural practice. Despite this, there always seemed to be an unresolved conflict between their background

Figure 2 Sarah Carr (*née* Johnson – my Grandmother) photographed at Whitley Bay 1930

and their present social situation. It always felt strange to leave our four-bedroomed detached house at Whitley Bay, a fairly middle-class dormitory seaside town on the north-east coast, to travel to dust-covered Consett in our nice Rover or Opel Cadett in the late 1960s. The contrast between evenings where my parents would host dinner parties with beautifully prepared French cuisine and fine wine and afternoons of lovingly prepared cups of tea, angel cake and tinned salmon sandwiches felt strange. I felt I didn't fully belong in either environment, uncomfortable with the pretence of the one and the traditional, closeting feel of the other. The strange, exhilarating taste of foreign foods contrasted with the sickly feeling of eating too much white bread and cake.

Figure 3 Sarah Carr (*née* Johnson – my Grandmother) in service, dressed up in a chauffeur's uniform 1930

Therefore, this book uses my own background to show that popular culture is central to my family history, but in part rejected by my parents. I seek to reclaim my own family's material culture links with popular culture after an enforced 'hiatus' in which my parents – for the best reasons in the world – sought to distance themselves from it. This sense of being between two worlds is skilfully described by Margaret Atwood in her novel, *Cat's Eye* (1989). Without this experience and personal history I couldn't have written a sympathetic account of popular culture informed by academic debate. For a time I was trapped in what Tim Lott has so accurately described:

Uncommitted and struck through with uncertainties, I begin to try to make myself invisible. My normal extroversion is intimidated and bruised into careful muteness, in case I make a fool of myself. I fear that I will be found out. I realize with a shock that my idea about university – people sitting and trying to make sense of things for their own sake – is wildly wrong and outdated. My old perception, the one from my school ten years ago, has turned out to still apply. The world is about making up a story and sticking to it. The university is about passing exams, and convention, and a certain kind of forgetfulness (1996: 204–5).

However, writing this book has allowed me to overcome these uncertainties; it has given me a vehicle for telling my own story. Carolyn Steedman explores her own childhood and the place of working-class biography in *Landscape for a Good Woman* (1986), and writes: 'What a successful analyst might do is to give the analysand possession of her own story, and that possession would be a final act of appropriation, the appropriation by oneself of ones own history' (1986: 131). A similar point was made by Jackie Stacey in discussing her own oral history project around women's recollections of cinema attendance:

> The invitation to tell one's story to a researcher may offer the promise of being heard, recognized, and taken seriously. What makes this study particularly appealing as a 'confessional opportunity' is the way in which the act of confession itself elevates the material into significance. It thus offers the chance to (re)gain the (lost) status of certain emotions from the past. For what surfaces repeatedly in these narratives is the desire to recapture past pleasures which were either 'laughable' to begin with . . . or which have since lost their status (with marriage or maturity) (1994: 331).

This strange sense of alienation, of being between or beyond boundaries, has fruitfully informed the work of many political activists and creative practitioners and some academics. In the field of architectural and design history, Anthony King has used his own experiences of growing up and still living in a one-storey building to write his book, *The Bungalow* (1995). He observed in his Preface: 'In certain circles in Britain, though not in North or South America, continental Europe, Australia, Asia, Africa or anywhere else in the world where the word can be found, the very mention of the term "bungalow" is sufficient to raise a smile, or better, a smirk. For these essentially middle-class or bourgeois folk, there is something ridiculous, even distasteful about the word, even about the type of dwellings itself.' Ian Davis in *Dunroamin: The Suburban Semi and Its Enemies* (Oliver, Davis and Bentley 1981) recalled his first day of architectural training:

> . . . I handed my tutor the usual form indicating name, age and home address: Hillside Drive, Edgware, Middlesex. He read my form and gave me a probing stare, followed by: 'I take it that you live in one of Edgware's semi-detached houses?' My affirmative prompted the observation that I should make early plans to move to a more civilised address, such as Camden Town. Later the same morning the First Year were gathered together for an initial briefing on the course and modern Architecture in general. We were strongly recommended to find out about a Swiss architect called Le Corbusier, 'the greatest living architect in the world.' We were advised to read his books and visit his buildings as soon as possible. Thus, before our first coffee break, the process of indoctrination was well under way. . . . Therefore, there was a persistent dilemma in those early months of my architectural course as to who was correct – home or tutor? (Oliver, Davis and Bentley 1994: 27).

Penny Sparke in her Preface to *As Long As Its Pink: The Sexual Politics of Taste* writes about her experience of being a woman as driving her intellectual project:

> Motherhood, rapidly succeeded by the death of my own mother led to a sharply focused emotional understanding of the continuity of feminine culture and experience, passed down through generations. Unlike masculine culture, which is largely inherited through mainstream institutions, its feminine equivalent is handed down through such marginal domestic skills as knitting and sewing, as well as through the shared enjoyment of popular culture – in my mother's case, Hollywood films. I realised that my intuitive feelings about material culture had come through continuity rather than, as I had thought, disruption and change. My interest in the 'post-modern' and my suspicions of the 'modern' were consistent with a commitment to the continuity of feminine culture as it has been formed, and marginalised, over the last century and a half (1995: ix–x).

Another leading feminist design historian, Pat Kirkham, has touchingly and graphically described her '. . . route from china cabinets in a pit village to a major study of two designers of world stature . . .' (1995: 224) as being one of amalgamating the autobiographical with the academic:

... one of the pleasures of more 'personal' work for me today is the *direct* engagement missing in earlier years when I was struggling to find my way in terms of both subject matter and methodologies. However, such work also related to certain modes of address of the working-class culture in which I grew up, including what I would now label 'women's culture'. My debts, in this, and in the choice of certain subject matters, are due as much to that collective culture and to my parents, particularly my perceptive, articulate and feminist mother, as to my academic and Marxist mentors (1995: 208).

Cheryl Buckley has used her own life as part of a study of home dressmaking: '... I am writing about an activity which has special meaning for me as daughter and niece in a large family of women, several of whom made clothes at home' (1998: 157–8). Joanne Lacey has used her working-class background of growing up in Liverpool as the source for her research into the reception of Hollywood musicals in the 1950s (1999). The novelist and biographer Margaret Forster has written a brilliant account of her grandmother and mother's working-class experiences in *Hidden Lives: A Family Memoir* (1995). She argues that: 'Over and over again we get told stories by our parents and grandparents, and sometimes, if these stories are treated seriously and checked, that is all they turn out to be – stories, unsubstantiated and often downright contradicted by the actual evidence in records. But sometimes beneath the stories lurks the history of more than an ordinary person. Sometimes their story is the story of thousands' (1995:13).

It is among women and within the field of gender studies that a more revealing and complex set of issues has arisen. The lives used as a backdrop for this book are ordinary in the sense that Forster uses the term – they stand for the lives of many millions of women. But they are far from ordinary in the sense of being undistinguished or uninteresting. They are lives that represent the power of Hollywood in Britain over everyday behaviour and values – power dismissed as 'bad' by those who fear the Americanization of British culture, celebrated by those who look to America as a haven beyond the stuffiness they perceive or experience in Britain. I would certainly identify with the latter; my image of America filled the void I felt growing up between different boundaries in the 1950s and 1960s. As a 16-year-old, female clerk recalled in 1948: 'I suppose I became interested [in film] because I saw something different from everyday life, saw Americans with their glamorous clothes and I heard their different way of speaking, saw so many things that I had not the chance of ever seeing' (Mayer 1998: 102).

But, as Miller has argued: '... any attempt merely to read off consumption as "good" or "bad" seems to miss the key point of recent history' (1996: 30) – the key point being that a more inclusive but analytical and reflexive approach is what is needed. I intend here to take this different perspective and account for the influence of Hollywood beyond the screen using contemporary sources informed by the local and the global and the personal recollections of those who experienced it directly, and in doing so to produce an analysis from the inside.

Notes

1. I am thinking here particularly of Pat Kirkham, Angela McRobbie, Cheryl Buckley, Carolyn Steedman, Valerie Walkerdine and Joanne Lacey.

2. I use the term dis-ease here to demonstrate how illness is an indication of some deeper malady that needs to be addressed and faced. Modern medicine alone cannot cure such dis-ease. For a simple example of this approach see Louise L. Hay, *Heal Your Life*, Eden Grove Editions, Enfield, 1996.

3. For example, see Stuart Hall *et al.* (1992), who acknowledge this trend in relation to the social sciences in the introduction to *Modernity and Its Futures*: '... the remarkable growth of "reflexivity," both in common experience and in social science thinking. To regard social enquiry as a hesitant process and self-understanding in a rapidly changing world is a far cry from the view that social scientists must strive to reflect reality as it is in itself, formulating the inner essence of society in abstract scientific terms' (1992: 10–11). On the links between feminism and teaching see Charlotte Brunsdon, 'Pedagogies of the Feminine: Feminist Teaching and Women's Genres', in *Screen*, 32 (4) (Winter 1991): 364–81.

4. Elizabeth Wilson claimed in her essay, 'All the Rage' :

Strange that when so much else has changed there still exists such a strong hostility to fashion amongst so many radicals. No one objects to changing tastes in interior decoration; changing fashions in medicine, holidays, and food are hardly noticed as such, although none is devoid of the snobbery and competitiveness of which fashion is so often accused; the socialists feel no guilt for adding fashionable gadgets – videos for example – to their long list of worldly goods. Ideas and preoccupations at least of the academic left are highly sensitive to fashion; and although changing fashions in ideas are usually justified in terms of some higher truth, the justification often amounts to little more than the *Vogue* cry: 'It's so Right for Now!' – The Austere Beauty of Habermas slashed with a Daring Touch of Baudrillard maybe (Gaines, J. and Herzog, C. (eds) 1990: 29).

See also Cook, P., *Fashioning the Nation: Costume and Identity in British Cinema*, BFI, London, 1996: 41.

5. Statistic published by *Times Higher Education Supplement*, 3 July 1998, pp.18–19.

6. It should be noted that this volume did discuss popular culture, but in a surprisingly dismissive way that is contrasted with the earlier, more inclusive but largely unacknowledged work of the Independent Group in Chapter 3.

7. Weeny boppers consisted of two balls on the end of springs that were attached to a head band. Wearing these objects made one look like a creature from outer space or a humanoid insect. They were mainly popular with children in the summer of 1982.

8. Paul Robeson lived and worked in Britain from 1928 to1939, starring in stage productions of *Showboat* and appeared in six British films. See Jeffrey Richards, 'Paul Robeson: The Black Man as Film Hero', in Barr, C. (ed.): 1986: 334–40.

9. It should be noted that fox-hunting is a pursuit that involves all classes of society in the north of England, based more on a shared, rural identity and working than on strict class divisions. Following the hunt on foot was free and open to all.

10. Now part of the University of Newcastle.

The Jazz Age: American Ascendancy and the Début of Deco

A rt deco is a term commonly used by design historians, dealers and collectors for a style of architecture and design prevalent during the period 1925 to 1939, the period when Classical Hollywood Cinema was established and the United States took the world lead in creating a consumer culture.[1] Art deco as a potent style in the American home and export markets became a powerful symbol of transatlantic glamour. In this chapter the origins of Hollywood glamour are explored in terms of Parisian *haute couture* and the 1925 *Exposition des Arts Décoratifs et Industriels Modernes*. The manner by which the art deco style was transposed to signify growing American prosperity and British post-colonial anxiety and class differences will then be compared.

Hollywood Arises

The fledgling film industry had emerged during the 1890s in America and Britain, with news or comedy shorts being shown as a novelty to vaudeville or music hall audiences (Eyles 1997). From 1900 films could be viewed in amusement arcades in America, and by 1905 separate areas were screened off in the arcades or in shops to create rudimentary viewing theatres. They were known as nickelodeons in American and penny-gaffs in Britain, because of their cheap entry price, and attracted a predominately working-class audience, squeezed on to narrow wooden benches in converted shops with blacked-out windows (Peiss 1986; Elsaesser and Barker 1990). The early cinemas were hugely popular – there were two hundred in Manhattan alone by 1907 – and they attracted working-class men, women and children of all races. This cheap, mass entertainment also spawned an early cult of glamour and star worship amongst female sections of the audience. Fan magazines were introduced in 1908 in America, and posters advertising the films on the street played to audience aspirations to glamour and fantasy. The one- and two-reel films drew on the conventions of variety and popular melodrama, often with *risqué* depictions of women in various states of undress or lingering embraces and kisses between heterosexual couples. Before the First World War audiences were as likely to view a film from France or Britain as they were an American product. In America, films were made in the urban ghettos of Chicago and New York. However, whilst the business and commercial interests of the film companies remained in New York, the burgeoning production process shifted to the West Coast from 1907 onwards. The main attractions were the clement weather, the clear light, and the wealth of various locations, from desert to mountain to beach to city, all within easy travel. Added incentives for this shift were the cheap, non-union rates expected by the on-set workers and distance from the demands of the commercial managers (Sklar 1994). Major new production companies like Zukor's Famous Players, which was to become Paramount Pictures, settled there before the First World War and were inspired by the myth of the great American West, of the move ever westward epitomized by the California Gold Rush, which had taken place only fifty years before. The geographic distance also fuelled the myth of Hollywood as the land of opportunity and of scandalous behaviour. By the early 1920s Hollywood, a small suburb of Los Angeles, was being used as a synonym for the American motion picture industry.

By the early 1920s America had come to dominate cinema screens on both sides of the Atlantic. The United States was undergoing prodigious economic expansion and maturing into a dominant world power to challenge Britain and Germany. America had emerged from the First World War into an economic boom; during the 1920s unemployment hardly rose above 5 per cent, and manufacturing output increased by almost one-third (Dimbleby and Reynolds 1988: 97). Consumption burgeoned, as did cinema attendance; by 1925 there were approximately 4,000 cinemas or other venues to view films in Britain and 22,000 across the USA (Dickinson and Street 1985: 10). The vaudeville-inspired one-reel short had been supplanted by the multiple-reel feature film with gripping narrative. In 1921 an early example of the enticing blend of glamour, sensuality and Parisian *haute couture* to be aimed at women was the blockbuster, *The Sheikh*. Starring controversial male matinée idol Rudolph Valentino, it drew upon the potent imagery of Orientalism (Studlar 1996; Bernstein and Studlar 1997). In fashion terms the most influential creator of the oriental look was Paris-based Paul Poiret. His loose-fitting gowns in rich fabrics, trimmed with fur, gems and feathers, were primarily designed for the stage just before the First World War, but acquired international renown during the early 1920s. He undertook a lecture tour of America in 1923 that provoked outrage and intrigue. The Western construction of Orientalism that informed his work and its reception was also transmuted into the creation of the vamp in Hollywood films, as seen for example in *Blood and Sand* (1920) starring Nita Naldi or the various productions of Cleopatra and Salome with stars such as Pola Negri and Theda Bara.

By the early 1920s the look of Hollywood films was more sophisti-cated – the pre-First World War approach to set design and costuming was to emulate the techniques used in production for the stage, with simple painted backdrops and contemporary clothes provided by the actors and actresses themselves. However, by 1920 new professional art directors were producing three-dimensional sets with rooms con-structed in rows, and studios were setting up separate costume depart-ments. The creation of a particularly rich *mise-en-scène* and glamorous costumes contributed to the mass appeal of Hollywood cinema. As the British architect Edward Carrick observed in 1930: 'Art Director is the name generally given to him who designs, furnishes, decorates and arranges the scenes or backgrounds of a film in harmony with the general characteristics of the drama which is being represented, so that its atmosphere and artistic qualities help the action to register senti-ments among the audience' (Carrick 1930: 440). By the late 1920s sound was a regular part of all feature-length films, replacing an orchestra playing accompanying music. *Our Dancing Daughters* (1928) was the first MGM film to include a pre-recorded musical soundtrack, while *The Jazz Singer* (1927) is the best-known American work to have incorporated sound.

Attending the cinema to see the 'talkies' was hugely exciting. My paternal grandmother saw *The Jazz Singer* in Newcastle at the time of its released in 1927, and kept a postcard commemorating the event throughout her life in her china cabinet. The introduction of the talkies was less positive for other members of my family. As my father recounted: 'In Leeds my grandfather, who had been a musician in the army, conducted and arranged music for a small pit orchestra at a music hall theatre. When they began to show films in the hall, at first they were silent movies and the orchestra played background music. When "talkies" took over my grandfather lost his job and never worked again.

My grandmother then began to work as a cleaner at a local tailoring factory' (Massey 1998).

With the technological advances of the adoption of sound came the erection of purpose-built cinemas and the conversion of older cinemas to relay sound. The late 1920s also witnessed a sophistication of roles, one of the most important being that of art director. One of the most successful art directors, whose career spanned the entire Classical Hollywood era, was Cedric Austin Gibbons, born in Brooklyn in 1890 and winner of three Oscars for art direction. His architect father, Austin Patrick Gibbons, tutored him in the workings of an architect's office. Austin Patrick Gibbons ran his own architectural practice based in New York City; it had been founded by his father on his arrival in New York from Ireland.

The young Gibbons spent a year travelling in Europe, and began collecting art and architectural books, which he continued to do throughout his career – donating over 4,000 volumes to Metro-Goldwyn-Mayer (MGM) when he retired in 1956. He studied at New York's Art Students League for four years before working for his father as a draughtsman. However, he found the technical aspects of architecture too challenging and, just before the First World War, was apprenticed to one of the first art directors in the movie industry, Hugo Ballin. Ballin was a mural and portrait painter, and also designed sets for the theatre and for the New York-based Edison Manufacturing Company, an early film production outfit. Gibbons maintained a simple approach to designing for film, by contrast with the dominant tendency, which was to reproduce the cluttered grandeur of the theatrical backdrop. Gibbons worked as an assistant for Edison at the New Bedford Studios in New York during 1915, introducing features to set designs that enhanced the film action. For example, when early film actors removed their gloves they had to pin them to the canvas backgrounds or flats, so Gibbons introduced three-dimensional mantelpieces to add verisimilitude, emulating contemporary practice in theatre design. In 1916 Gibbons joined Samuel Goldwyn just after the latter had left Famous Players-Lasky, to form Goldwyn Pictures Corporation in Fort Lee, New Jersey. He was supervising art director, with almost 100 films to his credit. His film career was interrupted by war service during 1917–18, when Goldwyn relocated to California, where Gibbons joined him after the war to work designing sets for Goldwyn's films, including those starring Geraldine Farrar. In *The Slim Princess* (1920) Gibbons created a fantasy set scaled down in size to emphasize the rotundity of the actors. The fantasy background also enhanced the narrative, as Jerome

Lachenbruch commented in 1921: '. . . the farcical story has a setting in which anything ridiculous may happen and still seem real. In other words, the beholder is prepared to accept the fairy tale because his imagination has been inducted into a receptive attitude by the romantic implications of the settings' (Lachenbruch 1921: 205).

When MGM was created in 1924 out of a merger of Goldwyn Pictures, Metro Pictures and Loew's Incorporated, Gibbons signed a contract ensuring that he would be named as art director on every film the company made in America: hence he appears in the credits of the majority of MGM films over the next 32 years. Donald Albrecht characterized the organization as: '. . . America's most prestigious and financially stable studio of the 1930s, MGM did produce Hollywood's largest body of modernist sets, which succeeded on the levels of broad concept, minute details, and exceptionally well-realized execution' (1986: 88). Cedric Gibbons orchestrated the design of the sets for MGM successes such as the sleek Greta Garbo showcases, *The Kiss* (1929) and *Susan Lennox: Her Fall and Rise* (1931), the historical fantasy *Marie Antoinette* (1938), the colourful flight of fancy *The Wizard of Oz* (1939) and the science fiction classic *Forbidden Planet* (1956). Albrecht describes the sets as modernist; however, they are more closely allied in design and decoration to art deco. Gibbons appropriated the Parisian art deco style to enhance the plots of two 'flapper films' starring Joan Crawford during the late 1920s.

Deco, Decadence and *Our Dancing Daughters*

Austin Gibbons travelled to Paris in 1925 and viewed the Exposition there with enthusiasm, This influence can be discerned in the 1928 film *Our Dancing Daughters*, designed with the help of designer Richard Day as Unit Art Director, in which the art deco style made its début.[2] Although the film was subsequently recorded as being filmed entirely using art deco sets, this was not the case (Mandelbaum and Myers 1985). Art deco was used for the homes of two characters, Diana Medford (Joan Crawford) and Anne (Anita Page) – the rest of the action taking place in more conventional Spanish Colonial Revival style surroundings. Gibbons was aware of the importance of the film set as a complement to the narrative and to the actors. In 1937 he stated: 'The stage setting surrounds the actors. In the movies, *once the scene is filmed*, you might almost say that the actors surround the set. Except in distant shots, the people are always in the foreground, the sets are but backgrounds against which they play. . . . The designer, in short, might be compared to a right-handed tennis player who has to be able to use the racquet equally well with his left hand' (Eustis 1937: 791). The deco style in this film signifies fast and easy living, the new amorality of youth during the jazz age. Crawford was already associated with such a lifestyle, named as a co-respondent in at least two divorce cases and winner of eighty-four trophies for dancing the Charleston and the shimmy: she was dubbed the 'Hey-hey, Charleston kid' (Tapert 1998: 44). This important ingredient of Hollywood glamour, that the off-screen life of the stars should be as exciting as the on-screen performances, certainly applied in the case of Crawford. Her ability to dance new-style flapper routines is central to the film. Her short, shingled hair style and dresses that reached above the knee reinforced the flapper image.

The opening sequence of *Our Dancing Daughters* consists of a close-up of Crawford's Charleston-dancing legs, surrounded by mirrors. On her nimble feet she wears silver dancing shoes, to quote the director of the film: '. . . shoes are the articles of wearing apparel that best reflect the character and personality of the wearer . . . Dancing slippers of a futuristic and cubistic design . . . gave the impression we wished to convey to the audience of the character' (BFI, Pressbook 1928). The surprise comes when underwear and then a dress are slipped on over the elegantly shod feet and dancing legs, prompting speculation that Joan Crawford was dancing naked except for her silver slippers and stockings. Similarly, in the party scene where Crawford performs the Charleston on the table she removes her skirt and dances only in her underwear, covered by a dress made up of strings of beads (Figure 4). For the film's showing in Stanley, Philadelphia, censors cut '. . . the close-up of Miss Crawford's undergarments on duty, the peeling off of her skirt while Charlestoning for her crowd . . . and a rather heavy love scene along the shoreline' (American *Variety*, 17 October 1928). The references to jazz music, black dancing and wild parties in the film reinforced the image, constructed through the national media, of Hollywood as a hedonistic and morally bankrupt town. This was further reinforced by the deco designs of the two women's homes.

The house of Crawford's character is designed on a vast scale, with a huge entrance hall and a sweeping staircase adorned by a Brancusi-type sculpture. The floor is reflective, and black; strong, sweeping parallel lines profile the room entrances and the curving staircase. There are geometric wall lights and full-length mirrors in the entrance. The lounge of the set has a shiny, black floor that reflects the various sources of lighting – three table-lamps, two wall-lights and a central overhead

Figure 4 Still from *Our Dancing Daughters* – Anita Page

light constructed from stepped, reflective metal (Figure 5). The stepped, ziggurat motif is continued on the arms of the settee at the far end of the room and the all-white fireplace surround. Circular shapes are also repeated in terms of a black circular rug and a drinks table, with quarter circles for the arms of the chairs. The dressing-room used by Diane (Crawford) and her mother consists of one illuminated wall with exotic bottles of perfumes delicately arranged on glass shelves. The home of Anne (Anita Page) is similarly lavish, with a stepped screen decorated with gold squares, framed by geometric wall lights with a chaise-longue and two sensuously curved chairs.

Anne and Anita's environments provide a contrast to that of the millionaire Ben Blaine (Johnny Mack Brown) in his rural retreat and to the Spanish Colonial Revival surroundings of the party, complete with galleon frescoes. Meaning was also conveyed through the style of the actor's clothing. Diana is transformed into a respectable and acceptable partner for Blaine, a change symbolized by her losing her 'flapper' dress and donning a more conventional evening gown. Her rival Anne has tricked Blaine into courtship, falsely proclaiming in the inter-titles that: 'I know I seem stupid – I can't be daring – and free

Figure 5 Still from *Our Dancing Daughters* – Joan Crawford's Home

with men – I'm not a "modern".' It is interesting to note that the credits for the inter-titles and the story all go to women, which was common at the time of Hollywood's infancy, before writing for the screen became more respectable. Anne finally meets her just deserts at the end of the film when, drunk and still attired in her 'flapper' dress, she teeters at the top of the stairs at the club where the party was held. She challenges the three cleaners at the bottom of the flight, scrubbing the floor in formation, as to why they are working, asking whether they have beautiful daughters they can marry off to rich men. This is greeted by a close-up of one cleaner shaking her head disapprovingly. Anne then falls down the stairs to her death, an ending characteristic of many films in the 'fallen women' category of the melodramatic genre, according to Jacobs (1995).

Our Dancing Daughters (1928) was a huge success in America and Britain; in fact, the story was serialized in the Hearst-owned newspapers at the time of the film's release in the US. It was most noted for the novelty of its art deco sets, designed by Gibbons, and for its *risqué* depiction of the young's decadent lifestyle. *Variety* noted:

> Booked in here for two weeks, 'Daughters' may be able to go three. The picture did around $40,000 on the week end, had a big Monday matinee and that night at 9.30 they were five deep behind the last row with standees to the doors on one side of the lobby. As a program leader it's been doing heavy business around the country. After taking a look – in fact two looks – there's reasons.
>
> This jazz epic follows the title a pip b.o. name in itself, is sumptuously mounted, gets plenty of playing from three girls and is sufficiently physically teasing in undress to do the trick (American *Variety*: 1928).

Another newspaper accentuated the novelty of the art deco sets:

> The setting is ultra and neo. If the players depict the development of flapperism, their environment is not lagging. We believe it is the first time that the screen has shown such a faithful picture of the great revolution the French mode in home furnishings is about to effect. The moderniste motif is carried out even to architectural details, and it will afford no end of keen amusement to see square, solid, severe lines and the quixotism of strange lighting arrangements (as quoted in Heisner 1990: 77).

The film's popularity and its impact as a vehicle for the representation of the glamorous flapper lifestyle can be gauged from its being the only film to be specifically mentioned twice in Chapter Three of the important Herbert Blumer book, *Movies and Conduct* (1933). The book was significant, as it formed part of a far-reaching study carried out under the aegis of the Motion Picture Research Council (MPRC). Alarm about the impact of Hollywood cinema on 'impressionable' sectors of society, particularly youth and women, reached new heights with the publication of the Payne Fund studies, particularly an alarmist summary that appeared in the mass-circulation magazine, *McCall's*, in 1932. This five-year study, entitled *Motion Pictures and Youth*, was executed by leading psychologists and sociologists. Its main findings were that the effects of picture viewing varied with age and social class, and that largely film viewing reinforced existing ideas and attitudes. However, this was not the result the MPRC wanted; and so a more sensationalized summary of the studies was published. Written by the former news editor of the *Literary Digest*, Henry James Forman, *Our Movie-Made*

Children, published in 1933, extracted parts from the Chicago interviews by Associate Professor of Sociology Herbert Blumer that accentuated delinquency, crime and sexual impropriety. In Chapter Three of Blumer's book, 'Imitation by Adolescents', *Our Dancing Daughters* is the only film to be specifically mentioned twice. One interviewee: 'Female, 16, white, high-school junior' admitted: '. . . I remember after having seen "Our Dancing Daughters" with Joan Crawford, I wanted a dress exactly like one she had worn in a certain scene. It was a very "flapper" type of dress, and I don't usually go in for that sort of thing' (p. 32). Indeed, alarmingly for the American guardians of decency, Blumer found that in 458 high-school student autobiographies, 62 per cent reported imitating some aspect of film star dress. But emulation went beyond dress. Another of the autobiographies revealed a seventeen-year-old who had tried:

> . . . in many ways to adopt the mannerisms of my favourite actress, Anita Page. My first realization of this was after I had seen her picture entitled 'Our Dancing Daughters'. This picture, as well as Anita Page, thrilled me as no other picture ever has or ever will. She didn't take the part of the good and innocent girl, but she was the cheat and the gold-digger. One would think that the leading man would never 'fall' for that type of girl, but he certainly did. Many a time I have tried to tilt my head, as she did, and wear my hair in back of my ears, and even stand in front of the mirror going through the same actions again (p. 43).

Our Dancing Daughters was so popular that it was followed by a sequel, *Our Modern Maidens*, in 1929. Again the sets were designed by Gibbons, drawing not only on art deco sources but also more traditional styles when the narrative demanded it. The costumes were by Albert Greenberg, or Adrian as he was known professionally, who had joined MGM in 1928, introducing another key element of what made up Hollywood glamour during the 1930s. He was to construct individualized, glamorous images for Greta Garbo, Jean Harlow, Norma Shearer and Joan Crawford; he designed everything Crawford wore on screen and the greater part of what she wore off screen from 1929 until 1943. He was brought to Hollywood by the wife of Rudolph Valentino, Natasha Rambova, and designed costumes for two of Valentino's films in 1925, *The Eagle* and *Cobra*. He remained at MGM until 1942, when he opened his own select shop in Beverley Hills, from where he continued to supply designs for Hollywood films. In *Our Modern Maidens*, his well-tailored, figure-skimming gowns decorated with luscious jewels perfectly

Figure 6 Still from *Our Modern Maidens* – Crawford Dancing

complemented the contemporary look of Joan Crawford. The lifestyle afforded by the age of modernity is depicted in the opening minutes of the film, with Joan Crawford again taking the starring role as ambitious Billie Brown, and being transported through the streets in an open-top car in the dead of night following a party. The radio is referred to, as is advertising and jazz music. The party of girls travel by train and are shown gambling and drinking – 'Lunch is poured', for example. The decadent lifestyle reaches new heights in Crawford's home, where she is depicted at a wild 4 July party dancing in exotic split skirt and bikini top (Figure 6). The home is pure deco, with imposing doorway framed by cog-like decoration, echoing the rhythm of the spiral staircase and vertical columns. The houseguests are seated on plush, drum chairs, bar-stools, or even a black PVC couch. Lights and mirrors again play a significant role, with the same stepped wall-lights as were used in *Our Dancing Daughters*, a huge mirror placed above the fireplace and a reflective floor covering. In the smaller rooms of the house doors are decorated with contrasting circles; there are stepped

Figure 7 Still from *Our Modern Maidens*

uplights, low chairs and luxurious dressing tables (Figure 7). The reflective flooring is decorated in contrasting circles of stark black and white. In this scene Billie introduces her family to Kentucky (played by Anita Page). Note the deliberate contrast between the floor-length, flouncy evening gowns of the seven women on the left, complete with elbow-length white gloves, and the dress worn by Crawford, which rises at the front to the knee, and Kentucky's sophisticated, knee- length day dress. Billie Brown's planned marriage to Gil (played by Douglas Fairbanks Jr) takes place; but revelations from her best friend, Kentucky, who has slept with Gil and may be pregnant, cause Billie to walk out on the marriage. She does so with a certain style: when the time comes to leave for the honeymoon, she chooses to leave alone, and announces to the assembled cameramen that this is now what modern couples do. The inter-title asks: 'Is this a modern moral . . . or just another immoral modern?' Again, the term modern is used to denote question- able morals and daring behaviour on the part of women in the film, and, once more, the film ends with a just reward for those who follow the rules. Billie annuls the marriage to Gil and is found in Paris by Abbott, the wealthy and influential diplomat whom she used to get her first husband his job in the American Embassy there.

The questionable morals of modernity linked with the scandalous behaviour of the young depicted in films such as *Our Dancing Daughters* and *Our Modern Maidens* inflamed extreme reactions in Britain and America. In the US this led to the adoption of the Production Code in 1930, covered in Chapter 2; but a swifter reaction came from the British Parliament in 1927, with the passing of the Cinematograph Film Act. The Act attempted to limit the quantity of imported American films and boost the British film industry by imposing quotas for their exhibition. Before 1909 the British were at the forefront of film production and the manufacture of projection and camera equipment. However, by 1920 only 15 per cent of films screened in Britain were British in origin. This was largely due to the American decision in 1909 to market and distribute their products effectively abroad, with Britain as the prime target. By 1925 there were 22,000 cinemas in the USA and 4,000 in Britain, with screenings dominated by a more integrated and powerful Hollywood industry selling more attractive products (Street 1997). By 1925 only 5 per cent of films shown in Britain were British-made. The 1927 Act was largely a futile gesture, triggered by the all-pervasive popularity of American films in Britain. But it was not only the questionable moral aspects of the films or the economic ramifications that gave rise to the Act – it was a general anxiety about the declining importance of Britain as a global power and the corresponding ascendancy of America.

America had emerged from the First World War: '. . . with a great capital surplus and owning much of the world's gold; in order to sell abroad it had to transfer wealth to potential buyers' (Godden 1998: ix). Emily Rosenberg in *Spreading the American Dream* (1992) characterized the 1920s thus: '. . . the United States flooded the world with products, branch plants and investment capital . . . making the decade one of the most economically expansive in the nation's history' (1992: 122). For the first time in the twentieth century America challenged British dominance in the markets of the British Empire and the home market itself. America's share of all world exports rose to 16 per cent by 1929, whilst that of Britain declined to 12 per cent. Ordinary Americans enjoyed a higher standard of living than their British counterparts, exploiting new technologies in everyday life, with one in five owning a car by 1929, compared to one in fifty Britons (Chant 1989). The success of the American economy was sustained in the 1920s by the sale in foreign markets of new types of consumer goods that exploited new technologies, like vacuum-cleaners and tyres, while Britain relied more on the heavy, traditional industries of coal-mining, shipbuilding, iron and steel production and textiles. Britain had led the Industrial Revolution in the eighteenth and nineteenth centuries, but that position of power was now occupied by America as the leader of a second industrial revolution of Modernity. Because this wave of Modernity came from America it was perceived as an import and also as a threat to the 'civilized' values of the British Empire. The British elite felt threatened by the ascendancy of America during the 1920s. The British Empire Exhibition at Wembley in 1924–5, according to the *Pocket Guide* on sale at the time, was an attempt:

> To find, in the development and utilisation of the raw materials of the Empire, new sources of wealth. To foster inter-imperial trade, and open fresh world markets for Dominion and home products. To bring the different races of the British Empire into closer and more intimate association, and to demonstrate to the people of Great Britain the almost illimitable possibilities of the Dominions, Colonies, and Dependencies overseas (1924: 2).

The exhibition was a huge undertaking, at a total cost of $4.5 million (US), which attracted 17.5 million visitors to its 216-acre site in 1924. This desire on the part of government to reassert the power of the British Empire was matched by a move to limit the exhibition of Hollywood films in Britain and gradually build up the production of British film for distribution to the rest of the Empire.

Consequently, in 1928 7.5 per cent of films shown in British cinemas had to be British. This in fact led to a higher concentration on the production of fewer, higher- quality American films. The British market was invaluable for Hollywood, providing 30 per cent of Hollywood's foreign gross profits, exceeding 30 million dollars (US) annually by 1936. The impact of the films is difficult to exaggerate. Tim Lott lucidly described the childhood experience of his father during the 1920s in his autobiographical novel, *The Scent of Dried Roses*: 'But it was the cinema that thrilled Jack's – and every other child's – imagination more than anything else – the first great hustle by another culture into the isolated life of England which, up until this point, had remained a unique, peculiar and yet essentially European place' (1996: 49). The films carried with them powerful images of American consumer goods, which, as the American authorities were completely aware, British film audiences found highly desirable. According to Vasey: 'As early as 1922 the U.S. Department of Commerce had coined the slogan "trade follows the motion pictures", and its spokesmen were fond of repeating the somewhat arbitrary claim that for every foot of film exported, a dollar was earned for the United States in spin-off sales of other goods' (1997: 42). In 1926 a Motion Picture Section was established within the Specialities Division of the Department of Commerce. In 1928 the secretary of the most significant trade organization for the film industry at that time, the Motion Picture Producers and Distributors of America, told a conference of salesmen that: 'the motion picture has dropped into your laps a selling agency, the like of which you advertising experts never even dreamed of. People are going to the motion picture as to an animated catalogue for ideas of dress, of living, of comfort' (as quoted in Vasey 1997: 43). Hollywood was also willing to accommodate the wishes of British censors: 'for example British requirements were sometimes idiosyncratic. Jack Vizzard maintains that the British insisted on twin rather than double beds in all circumstances. This stipulation was not required by American censors but was usually accepted for the sake of British distribution' (Vasey 1997: 146).

So American films were perceived as a threat to Imperial values by the British elite, but as a source of great entertainment and a window on to a world of fashion, glamour and hedonism for the majority of the British population. Ironically, this leadership of glamour had been achieved through the appropriation of Parisian *haut couture* and the expensive, luxurious style of art deco, which was first seen by an influential group of Americans when they visited the Parisian *Exposition des Arts Décoratifs et Industriels Modernes* in 1925.

It should be stressed at this point that the style was not known as art deco at the time. This was a generic term first used in 1966 in the Paris Musée des Arts Décoratifs exhibition, which focused on the style of the 1925 Paris *Exposition des Arts Décoratifs et Industriels Modernes*, from where the two words 'art' and 'deco' were derived. The term entered popular usage with the publication of Bevis Hillier's book, *Art Deco of the Twenties and Thirties*, in 1968. Art deco was adopted as an overarching label for objects that were not avant-garde and Modernist, but were at once modern, revivalist and decorative. Art deco signified the orientation toward luxury, glamour and expensive decoration characterized by the 1925 Paris exhibition. It also reflected a late-1960s interest in the decorative and the surface developed in the light of nascent post-modernism in architecture and design. The exclusive end of the 'antique' art deco market featured pricey Cartier watches, Lalique glass or Ruhlmann furniture, and a spate of publications followed, filled with glossy photographs of expensive, hand-made objects or luscious buildings and interiors. But such has been the craze for art deco since 1968 that all manner of objects in vaguely deco style are collected and admired – from 'vintage' handbags to plastic cigarette cases. The style has recently been the subject of serious academic discussion, most notably Tag Gronberg's *Designs on Modernity: Exhibiting the City in 1920s Paris* (1998), which places the spectacle of the 1925 exhibition within the context of modernity. Hollywood's appropriation of art deco in the 1920s marks one of the last moments that Paris was to define popular glamour during the twentieth century.

The Migrations of Glamour

The concept of glamour, of a particular look or style being the source of envy, aspiration and desire, only entered common usage during the twentieth century. A relatively new addition to the English language, its meaning in the eighteenth century was linked with magic, enchantment, necromancy or a sorcerer's spell. One of the earliest recorded uses was in 1721 in a Scottish verse: 'When devils, wizards or jugglers deceive the sight, they are said to cast glamour o'er the eyes of the spectator' (*Oxford English Dictionary*: 1933). The term was linked with the power of the occult, something with such a fascinating and attractive power that it could not be real (Tapert 1998). In *Roget's Thesaurus of English Words and Phrases* (1962) the word is categorized with beauty, prestige and: '. . . *spell*, charm, glamour, enchantment, cantrip, hoodoo, curse, evil eye, jinx, influence; bewitchment, fascination' (1962: 395). Linked primarily with feminine allure, narcissism and the rise of mass consumption, it embodies a fascinating contradiction.

A glamorous face or dress can be attractive and alluring when seen from afar, but close up and in detail the inherent magic disappears and something more ordinary is revealed. Glamour of the Classical Hollywood period relied on creating a glowing image for the female star – the convention of three types of lighting, key, fill and back, established by the 1920s, created a virtual aura around the female stars (Dyer 1997: 87). The white glow of the Caucasian, female film star is a central aspect of Hollywood glamour. The backlighting in particular eradicates shadows and separates out the star on screen from the background with a halo effect. This mode of lighting was also employed in the glamour photographs of female stars during the 1930s and 1940s (Heisner 1990: 58). The use of light in the creation of glamour was further enhanced by hair gel, reflective materials for garments and mirrored surfaces used in set design and publicity shots. Indeed, MGM boasted they had more stars than the galaxy. The glimmer and shine of Hollywood is therefore a double-edged attribute. In Britain, Hollywood as a mythical place rather than a geographic location is still referred to in the popular media as 'Tinseltown' (Macaulay 1999: 45). This denotes the allure but also the perceived artificiality and ephemerality of Hollywood glamour. Shining stars are most fascinating when seen from afar. Audiences are just as intrigued by the scandals behind the glamour, the tawdry nature of life in Hollywood, the tarnish of the tinsel, the perilous nature of stardom. The opposing forces of the pleasure principle and the death drive, which Sigmund Freud was defining and developing contemporaneously with the growth of popular film, may offer one possible explanation in psychoanalytical terms (Freud 1961; Foster 1993). Subjects are drawn to that which they desire and are, by the same token, repulsed by it and wish to destroy or repress it. In terms of glamour this can only be resolved when the object of the fantasy dies, the more tragically the better, as in the case of Carole Lombard (killed in an aircraft crash 1942), Jean Harlow (died 1937 of kidney failure as a result of childhood illness), Marilyn Monroe (sleeping tablet overdose 1962) and Princess Diana (car crash 1997). The perception is that all the causes of death could be regarded as self-inflicted. Lombard was only on the aeroplane because her husband, Clark Gable, refused President Roosevelt's request to tour the country to sell national bonds. The myth of Jean Harlow's death during the filming of Saratoga (1937) revolves around her Christian Scientist mother, who, it is alleged, refused to allow the necessary blood transfusion, needed because the use of hair dye to achieve the platinum blond colour had caused cancer. She was replaced by a double, who was shot only from behind, to complete the film. Marilyn Monroe was also a victim of her own success: plagued by eating disorders, drug addiction and alcoholism she died alone, celebrated as recently as 1988 by Elton John in his eulogy, Candle in the Wind, which celebrated the frailty of the glamorous star. The song was reworked movingly for Princess Diana's funeral in September 1997 by Elton John as England's Rose in tribute to the most glamorous and tragic woman of the century. As Nicholas Mirzoeff has argued: 'The British Left, from which cultural studies originated, was so badly wrong about the Diana phenomenon precisely because of its profound distrust for images and appearance. By the time of her death, Diana had become a global visual icon . . .' (1999: 233).

An additional reading has been proposed by Gaylyn Studlar. In her 1990 essay, 'Masochism, Masquerade, and the Erotic' she proposes an analysis of glamour during the Classical Hollywood era informed by Deleuze's pre-Oedipal theory of masochism (Gaines and Herzog 1990: 229–49). The masochist subject fantasizes about the punishing mother figure who exhibits pseudo-sadistic behaviour. Studlar uses Marlene Dietrich to illustrate her argument, with the star using fur, white satin and black ostrich feathers to reveal but also conceal the flesh, framing the perfect, flawless white face with arched eyebrows and disdainful expression. Gaylyn explains:

> The suggestive power of the partially concealed body manifests the play of anticipation and suspense that structures masochistic temporality. Masochism obsessively recreates the suspended movement between concealment and revelation, disappearance and appearance, seduction and rejection, in emulation of the ambivalent response to the mother who the child fears may either abandon or overwhelm him. The control of desire through theatrical ritualization of fantasy in masochistic masquerade delays the genital consummation of desire, a sexual act that would restore the symbolic merger of mother and child (1990: 237).

Such an interpretation also offers a more active role for women as spectators beyond the constructed female role outlined by Laura Mulvey (1975). If glamorous actresses like Marlene Dietrich are playing out a masquerade and are in control of the situation, then a more powerful and self-aware role is possible for women on and off the screen. Hence glamour is a rich and subtle area for exploration, one that offers various roles and possibilities for men and women as spectators and actors. An advertisement in *Picturegoer* for the magazine *Woman's Fair: The Journal of Beauty*, which appeared on 16 April 1938, is informative at this point. The question is posed: 'What is this thing called glamour?' and the answer provided is: 'What makes some women so sparkling and alluring that they rival, in everyday life, the much-admired "glamour girls" of stage and screen? It isn't a matter of money. But it certainly is a matter of "knowing how" in all that concerns make-up and dress. Knowing one's type and knowing what therefore can and cannot be done when using cosmetics or choosing costumes' (p. 31). Therefore glamour offers the choice of expressing one's individuality, but in a knowing, sophisticated manner.

Glamour is normally regarded as suspect in academic discourse. This was aptly summed up by the music journalist Julie Birchill in the 1980s:

'. . . the left has been populated by drabbies who seem to equate glamour with conservatism; as though having a suntan and a good suit makes you an honorary member of the South African police force' (as quoted in Elms 1986: 12). As in the general academic debate around consumption, there are those who adamantly oppose the notion of glamour as an instrument of capitalism and those who celebrate it as oppositional subversion. Florence Jacobowitz and Richard Lippe argue (1992: 3):

> Glamour . . . has become a problematic site for feminist discussion. Too often theorists contend that it speaks of the fetishized objectifications of the woman within representation, epitomizing the appropriation of the woman's body for the gratification of male pleasure. Marxist interpretations of glamour, like the one offered by John Berger in *Ways of Seeing* (pp. 146–8) suggest that glamour is a capitalist invention used to feed the spectator's envy for a manufactured desire (which is always one step away from fulfilment). We wish to redress this intellectual embarrassment at the notion of glamour, but without recourse to camp. Glamour was important to many of the women's films, to the viewing audience and for a complex of reasons. Glamour perfectly addressed the characteristics for which these stars were greatly admired: it speaks of confidence, empowerment, and, depending on its use, articulates all that is *not* domestic, confined, suppressed. Glamour, above all, is not mundane.

The more general concept of fashionability as a an aspect of popular, material culture dates back at least to the turn of the century, when the dress and mores of the British Royal family were the source of ideas about what was fashionable and desirable in Britain. In Edwardian society, the Prince of Wales and his entourage set the style, mediated through new illustrated magazines and newsreels. *The Illustrated London News* and *The Sketch* carried images of race meetings and court events that displayed the aristocracy and the court circle at play. Narratives of gossip and luxury were also constructed in America through popular magazines and newspapers centring on the lives, the parties and marriages of East Coast high society. It was of course French style that led fashion and interior decoration at this point, through the purchase of Louis XV revivals and the hand-made finery of turn-of-the-century fashions, exemplified in Edith Wharton and Ogden Codman Jr's *The Decoration of Houses* (New York 1987 [1902]). Taste was led and the style set by the Vanderbilts and the Fricks on Park Avenue in New York. This turn-of-the-century taste was for the sophisticated, European ideal exemplified in the Italian Renaissance and eighteenth-century France.

Taste was also linked with social class, as Wharton and Codman confidently declared in their popular book: 'Vulgarity is always noisier than good breeding, and it is instructive to note how a modern commercial bronze will "talk down" a delicate Renaissance statuette or bust, and a piece of Deck or Minton china efface the color-values of blue-and-white or the soft tints of old Sevres' (1987 [1902]: 190). It is important to bear in mind that Edith Wharton, better known for her published novels, was born in New York into a distinguished and wealthy family, and privately educated at home and in Europe. She lived in France after her marriage in 1907 and mingled with a cosmopolitan elite, including Henry James. Similar beliefs about European style and good breeding informed other self-help books and articles during the early twentieth century in America. Other advice manuals and American magazines like *House and Garden* or *The Woman's Home Companion* emphasized the importance of grand historical styles and the furnishing of palatial interiors with French or English antiques.

Theatres built during the early twentieth century drew on such lavish French Second Empire styling. The Strand Theatre, New York, designed by Thomas Lamb, opened in 1914 and served to: '. . . inaugurate the new era in American picture house design with gilt and marble, deep pile rugs, crystal chandeliers hanging from the ceiling and original art works on the walls, with luxurious lounges and comfortable chairs, a thirty piece orchestra . . . and a mighty Wurlitzer' (Sharp 1969: 73). Although programmes at US theatres mingled variety acts with films, the public display of moving pictures had come a long way from their projection in temporary structures at fairgrounds or at the equally suspect nickelodeons. By the time of the First World War it had become acceptable to show films in city-centre theatres, designed in the ornate, *beaux arts* style: in other words, in glamorous surroundings. Indeed, the surroundings were deliberately so constructed in order to broaden the audience by attracting the more respectable working-class as well as middle-class viewers. The gorgeous decoration also related to the décor of the respectable and familiar department stores. As Jeanne Thomas Allen observed: 'In the 1920s the motion picture palace's aristocratic decor matched the proximity of film viewing to shopping areas as invitations to merge on-screen and off-screen surroundings' (in Gaines and Herzog 1990: 125).

By contrast, the avant-garde movements, which dominate design histories, were relatively little know at the time. The work of Charles Rennie Mackintosh, Adolf Loos or Peter Behrens was unfamiliar to most Europeans or Americans. What was familiar was the latest in Paris fashion as worn by the Royal Family in Britain or American dollar princesses. The sociologist Thorstein Veblen observed this monied class in America in *The Theory of the Leisure Class* in 1899, and coined the terms 'conspicuous leisure' and 'conspicuous consumption' to describe the pursuit of what he regarded as useless activities like breeding pedigree dogs or fashion. As Richard Godden (1998) has argued, these activities served to preserve the status quo, to deny change and to prolong a lifetime of obvious leisure in the traditionally decorated drawing-room of turn-of-the-century New York. Whilst the mass of the population could witness such displays of wealth and glamour in the department stores and in the pages of magazines or newspapers or in early film footage, they could not easily emulate the look. It relied on hand-made, expensive materials and highly skilled makers for its production and inherited social mores for its consumption. The likelihood is that even if members of the lower classes did manage to emulate their social superiors by means of home dressmaking or second-hand purchases, then, as the leading German sociologist, Georg Simmel commented in 1905: '. . . fashions are always class fashion, by the fact that the fashions of the higher strata of society distinguish themselves from those of the lower strata, and are abandoned by the former at the moment when the latter begin to appropriate them' (Frisby and Featherstone 1997).

However, by the time that Hollywood came to dominate the cinema screens and popular leisure culture of America and Britain in the 1920s glamour and fashionability converged, and a glamorous appearance was comparatively more attainable and democratic. Godden argues that economics and consumption had, by the 1920s, entered the 'sphere of reproduction' (1998: xxiii), with a high turnover of style typified by Hollywood film. Glamour had been modernized through mass production methods, synthetic materials and the commercialization of home craft skills such as dressmaking. While during the early twentieth century home craft skills were used to replicate some form of Arts and Crafts authentic, pre-industrial object, decoration or clothing, by the late 1920s they were used to replicate the dress of film stars or decorate homes to emulate the sets of Hollywood films. As Jeanne Allen has argued when discussing the film *Roberta* (1935): 'The film's presentation of the chief fashion designer as an American woman in Paris bears an intriguing relation to the history of French–American relations in film fashion design: In the teens, American film companies had hired Parisian designers, but the 1930s *Nation's Business* announced that the importation strategy had failed, that Parisian designers had returned to Paris, but that because of Hollywood's "1200-mile style parade" in film, it had become the world's fashion center' (Allen 1980: 493).

The trade journal's report of what this shift meant in ideological terms is closely matched in the film's inherent argument for social democratization through universal consumption. The 1937 article explains that '*la couture* used to consist of some 200 firms which employ over 300,000 people and which design clothes available at private showings to audiences which include the "Famous Forty", a group of social leaders, stage favourites, or members of royal families celebrated for their chic. The clothes they select become the clothes imitated and worn all over the world.' But 'by 1937, Hollywood actresses had come to influence world-wide tastes and choices far more than social leaders and members of the aristocracy' (Allen 1980: 493–4).[3]

A dominant theme of many classic Hollywood films is movement up the social ladder, signalled by the placement or passage of characters into settings like the luxury hotel, apartment, night club or ocean liner. But while the locus of this look, which apparently fed such aspirations and offered social mobility, came to be fixed in an American signification, the look itself was imported from the traditional home of the glamorous image, Paris.

Americans in Paris 1925

The 1925 Paris *International Exposition des Arts Décoratifs et Industriels Modernes* provided a principal source for the glamour of modernity. Tag Gronberg indicates that the exhibition was important for reinforcing Paris as the centre of the global luxury trade and women's *haute couture* fashion, using the new technology of lighting to create magnificent spectacles (1998). Most exciting for the visitors was a stroll by night over the Pont Alexandre 111. 'Along the Pont Alexandre 111, forty boutiques showcased an impressive range of Parisian luxury industries, with the products of haute couture predominating. This was an urban thoroughfare comprised entirely of brilliantly lit shop-windows in which the boutique defined not only *la rue* but also Paris itself' (1998: 33). The exhibition was visited by a huge party of 108 officials, manufacturers and designers from America on the invitation of the Secretary of Commerce, Herbert Hoover. The party included journalists from *The New York Times*, and members of the Association of National Advertisers, the American Society of Interior Designers (ASID), the American Institute of Architects (AIA) and the Architectural League of New York. The American designers Russel Wright, Donald

Figure 8 Ruhlmann Interior at 1925 Paris Exposition

Deskey and Walter Dorwin Teague also attended, along with thousands of other Americans. They returned to the United States, as they had done previously from earlier Expositions, with key ideas about the latest glamorous style and fashions. What the American visitors found in 1925 was that the revival of historical styles had waned, and a completely new and fresh style was in evidence. The ironwork of Edgar Brandt was much admired, with its repetitive, angular motifs, as was the sheer luxury of the upmarket department stores' ensembles and chic interiors, such as the *Pavilion of a Rich Collector*. Designed by Pierre Partout and furnished by the leading French *ensemblier* Emile-Jacques Ruhlmann, the sumptuous interior comprised sixteen rooms. The Grand Salon was furnished on a musical theme with a Gaveau grand piano veneered in exotic Macassar ebony and a ceiling mural by A. Rigal symbolizing Beethoven's symphonies (Figure 8). The stylized figures in this painting, with their exaggerated classical torsos, were of a realist style that certainly influenced American visitors and was reproduced in murals and carved on the walls of skyscrapers throughout the cities of the US. The room's luxurious mood was further enhanced by a massive central chandelier, silk-covered walls, and a specially commissioned wall painting of exotic female figures and parrots entitled *Les Perruches* by Jean Dupas. A reproduction of this painting later featured in the sets of Cecil B. de Mille's film *Dynamite* of 1929.

The style of the exteriors of the temporary pavilions was equally influential. They mingled a stripped-down classicism with ziggurat outlines and Egyptian details, incorporating decorative elements derived from Tutankhamun's tomb, discovered in 1922. This was true of the main façade of the *Pavilion of a Rich Collector*, with the imposing pillars of its main entrance the *Porte d'Honneur,* and also of the pavilion of the decorating firm, *La Maîtrise*, part of the major Parisian department store, Les Galeries Lafayette. Use of bold colours and shapes, ziggurat profile, sunburst motif, frozen fountain and exotic materials were all design elements that the party took back to the States.

At the time, the Americans referred to the style seen at the 1925 Exposition not as art deco but as art moderne, jazz modern or modernistic. Design historians have been eager to point out the differences between the mainstream pavilions, such as that of Partout and Ruhlmann, and the *Pavillon de L'Esprit Nouveau* by Le Corbusier. The former is treated as a symbol of old-world craft values and retrograde revivalism and the latter as the work of an enlightened modernist. However, it is important to stress that the Americans regarded modernism and so-called art deco as part of the same new style, a style that served the needs of a growing American economy and American world presence.

Deco, American Style

The look of the exhibits was communicated throughout America by means of newspaper and magazines features, exhibition displays and department store promotions, including exhibitions at Macy's, Lord and Taylor and Abraham and Straus. A selection of almost 400 objects, including furniture, glass, ceramics, metalwork and textiles, was made by Charles R. Richards, director of the American Association of Museums, from the 1925 exhibition and shown nation-wide, beginning at the Metropolitan Museum of Art, New York, early in 1926. It then toured to eight other city-centre museums. The Metropolitan Museum also opened a permanent gallery devoted to twentieth-century furniture, which was dominated by pieces purchased at the Paris Exposition. The 'modern' style, later identified as art deco, was used for urbane window displays, exhibitions and room settings in New York's leading luxury department stores. In 1928 Macy's used Robert W. de Forest from the

Metropolitan Museum as a consultant for their *An International Exposition of Art in Industry* exhibition. Installed by the New York stage designer, Lee Simonson, the showcases were adorned with setting-sun motifs and the angular backdrops in the display cases echoed the stark expressionism of the German film, *The Cabinet of Dr Caligari*, released in America in 1921. *An International Exposition of Art in Industry* was also significant as it included not only luxurious decorative arts from Paris by figures such as Maurice Dufrene, but also work by designers working in America like Kem Weber, which were comparatively simple, relying on motifs of aeroplanes, skyscrapers and dancers.

Weber had trained in his native Germany before settling in Santa Barbara after the First World War. He established his own interior design and furniture design studio in Los Angeles in 1921 and worked as Art Director for Barker Brothers from 1922 to 1927. He shot to fame after his inclusion in the *Art in Industry* exhibition and resigned from Barker Brothers to establish his own design studio in Hollywood in 1928. He produced *moderne* designs for silverware, clocks and furniture and also worked as a freelance art director for a number of the major studios. While the French goods were primarily aimed at the luxury market, their American derivatives were intended for mass consumption. As Simonson declared at the time of the exhibition: '... art in this age has to be simplified if it is going to be produced on a large enough scale for most people to afford and enjoy it'. The mass production of goods would create 'a tremendous widening of the variety of articles in everyday use as generally accepted essentials of modern life' (Meikle 1979: 25).

As the American designer of the Radio City Music Hall and visitor to the Paris Exposition, Donald Deskey, recalled in 1933: 'Out of the chaotic condition caused by an unprecedented era of prosperity and the overpublicising of contemporary architecture and decoration, following the Exposition of Decorative Arts in Paris in 1925, there emerged a style' (Deskey 1933: 266). Skyscrapers were a fitting motif for the new style in textiles being produced by American designers, for example Clayton Knight's *Manhattan* textile design of 1925–6. The multi-storey blocks also inspired the furniture designs of Paul T. Frankl, a German immigrant with a practice first in New York and then Los Angeles (Figure 9). An entire room designed by Frankl was exhibited by Macy's in its 1927 *Art in Trade* show. Frankl was inspired by the new speed of American city life, of the noise and random synchronism of Jazz music and dance. In his treatise on the skyscraper and modern design *Form and Re-Form* (1972 [1930]) he wrote: 'Today we find

Figure 9 Paul Frankl, Skyscraper Furniture

ourselves in the midst of a movement more active and more significant
than that ever experienced by any other nation. Out of manifold
experiments national unity begins to emerge. At last we are expressing
our own country and our own century' (1972: 1). Although many
Europeans were horrified at the noise, speed and frenetic pace of New
York, alluded to in Fritz Lang's dystopian vision *Metropolis* (1923), for
others it was experienced as and epitomized what was best in Modernity
– it seemed liberating for those *émigrés* from tradition-bound Europe,
where no skyscraper was built until after the Second World War.

New York, the commercial centre of America, was also the centre of art deco development in America. In a nation-wide survey conducted for the comprehensive *Rediscovering Art Deco U.S.A.* (Capitman, Kinerk and Wilhelm, 1994) the authors found 547 extant examples of art deco building in New York, a figure far outranking any other city in America. The volume of art deco building can be explained by the economic dominance of the city during the twentieth century as America expanded into a formidable world power. The building boom of the late 1920s used the latest style of art deco to express the new-found confidence and mood of expansion that dominated American life in the inter-war years. Skyscrapers were built to meet the 1916 zoning laws in New York, which determined the stepped-back appearance of these symbols of corporate America, so constructed to avoid plunging the streets below into permanent shade. The Barclay–Vesey Building (Ralph Walker for McKenzie, Voorhees and Gmelin, 1923) was erected for the New York Telephone Company, and drew on European avant-garde features, particularly the carved stone decoration that topped the brickwork pinnacles. The 56-storey Chanin Building (Sloan and Robertson, 1927), built for property developer Irwin Chanin, included art deco elements taken straight from the Paris exhibition, particularly the bronze and terracotta friezes that decorate the exterior of the second and fourth floors, using geometrized floors, scrolls and frozen fountain motifs. The wrought iron and bronze gates that bar the entrance to Chanin's fifty-second-floor private office also draw on French precedents, particularly the work of Edgar Brandt; the details, however, refer to American mechanical ingenuity and capital accumulation – the stylized sunburst is actually composed of machine cogs, and the base is made up of piles of coins. Brandt himself designed and made (in Paris) the doors and other metalwork adornments, 50 tons in all, for the Cheney Brothers (Howard Greenley, 1925) fabric store, exemplifying the importance of French design to the look of the New York skyscraper. Other key examples of art deco skyscrapers designed before 1930 for corporate America include the Chrysler Building (William Van Allen, 1928) for the automobile magnate Walter P. Chrysler, and the Film Center Building (Ely Jacques Kahn, 1928) for Buchman & Kahn (Figure 10).

The art deco style was also employed by architects in every American city during the pre-1929 boom era. From Chicago to Cincinnati art deco was the preferred style for the design of corporate buildings, hotels and apartment blocks. Second to New York in terms of sheer volume of art deco buildings was the new home of the film industry, Los Angeles in California. Early examples of French art deco-inspired building in

Figure 10 Empire State Building

boomtown Los Angeles include the Bullocks Wilshire Department Store (John and Donald Parkinson, 1928). The store's vice president and general manager, Percy Glen Winnett, visited the Paris Exposition in 1925 with Donald Parkinson and returned to Los Angeles with ideas about how a fashionable department store should look. The exterior of the steel-framed building is clad in beige terracotta and geometrically decorated with oxidized green copper. Although inspired by the high style of Paris, it was one of the first buildings to be designed with the motorist in mind. The 241-foot spire that crowns the building is picked out against the California skyline by a distinctive blue-green light that can be seen for miles around. The huge, plate-glass, street-level display windows were aimed at attracting the attention of the passing motorist, and the main entrance was at the rear by the Motor Court. A *porte-cochère* shielded customers arriving in their cars; its ceiling was decorated by Herman Sachs with a huge fresco entitled *Spirit of Transportation*, important because it features those new modes of transport that typified and inspired this era. The ocean liner, aeroplane, locomotive and zeppelin are depicted in deco style.

Links between European style and the design of the Bullocks department store did not stop at the original inspiration of the 1925 Paris Exhibition. The French designer Sonia Delaunay designed the rugs that adorned the floors of the ground-floor women's accessory department. The main designer of the lavish interiors was the German-born Jock Peters, who had trained in the offices of the modern architect, Peter Behrens. He emigrated to Los Angeles in 1923, and worked initially as an architect's draughtsman before becoming an art director with the Famous Players/Lasky Corporation from 1924 to 1927. Having left the film industry he formed a design partnership with his brother called Peters Brothers Modern American Design, and used his film experience to create the stunning interiors at Bullock's. These resemble film sets in their sensitivity to lighting, reflective surfaces and differently themed and gendered spaces. For example, the Perfume Hall's lighting panels were encased in vertical metal strips reaching right up to the ceiling, contrasting dramatically with the St Genevieve Rose Marble (Figure 11). The Fur Atelier on the second floor by Peters featured a tiered display stand for the mannequin, lit from above by four spotlights, framed by two fluted pilasters and backed by a huge mirror.

During its first week of opening in September 1929 the store was visited by over 100,000 would-be shoppers. The store, like Hollywood films, allowed luxury and glamour to enter the lives of everyone – if visitors could not afford to shop at the store, they could marvel at the splendour of the décor. Indeed, it became the place where Los Angeles inhabitants would buy their wedding or prom dress, as well as catering to the tastes of Beverley Hills millionaires and film stars (Davis 1996). Other important pre-1930 art deco buildings in Los Angeles include the Stock Exchange (Samuel Lunden with John and Donald Parkinson, 1929), co-designed by the architects of Bullocks Wilshire, and the Oviatt Building (Albert Walker and Percy Eisen, 1927). The clothes manufacturer James Oviatt, who had visited the 1925 Paris exposition, used the French glass designer René Lalique, in his only American commission, to design moulded elevator-door panels for this new store,

Figure 11 Fur Atelier, Bullocks Wilshire Department Store, Los Angeles

which sold exclusive haberdashery to men. The interior light fittings and wall and ceiling glass coverings were made in France and transported to Los Angeles.

The assimilation of art deco in America was therefore evident, particularly following the Paris 1925 Exposition. It expressed the ideals of a newly developing, economically powerful nation. The reception of art deco in Britain was rather less positive in the aftermath of Paris and 1925, particularly among design critics responding to the erection of American-financed or inspired buildings in the south of England. Americanized art deco was frequently dismissed as 'jazz modern' rather than the 'real modern' of the International Style. However, what was really at stake was the waning world power of Great Britain.

The British Reaction

A similar pattern of development in the identification of glamour with Hollywood and art deco took place in Britain as had occurred in America. Orientalism was as popular amongst British audiences as American up until the mid-1920s, when art deco as the representation of modernity took hold. The 1925 Paris Exposition reinforced France's leadership of the luxury end of the market, defining fashion in terms of expensive clothing and interior decoration. Art deco enjoyed limited popularity, mainly amongst the young, rich and aristocratic, during the 1920s in Britain. A sturdy, masculine and nationalistic Arts and Crafts mindset still prevailed among designers, and was reinforced by the activities of the Design and Industries Association (DIA). Liberty's was as popular as ever, and figures like William Lethaby were still highly influential. While art deco was enthusiastically received in America and reconfigured to meet that country's needs, it was regarded as suspect among practising designers in Britain. The British reception of the 1925 Paris exposition was frosty compared to that in America. Gabriel Mourey, writing in *The Studio* magazine, which served the professional world of architects, designers and decorators, criticized the French pavilions:

> Speaking generally, they have some serious defects, of which the principal is that they are not sufficiently French in character, and their proportions are not such as one might have wished. They are somewhat heavy and they are lacking as much in delicacy and elegance as in that harmonious simplicity which is one of the essential marks of the French genius. They are pretentious and dreary; they bear, to an exaggerated degree the mark of a far too conscious striving after originality, novelty at any price, and this deprives them of all charm (July 1925: 16, 19).

It should be remembered that the British pavilion attracted widespread criticism for its comparative conservatism in the international press. A nationalistic brand of the Arts and Crafts ethic dominated, as Britain faced decline as a world power. At the more popular end of the market, mass-produced 'Tudoresque' furniture and half-timbered, olde-worlde building was popular for the same reasons. There was a flight back into the cosy idyll of an imagined, pre-industrial Britain (Wiener 1992).

Luxurious art deco did inspire some building work during the 1920s in England as it had in America, particularly in London. Claridge's, decorated by Basil Ionides (1927), the Savoy Hotel and Theatre by Ionides (1929) and the Strand Palace Hotel by Oliver Bernard (1930) served the luxury trade. Claridge's had enjoyed the earlier fashionability of royal connections going back as far as George IV; it was rebuilt in 1898 to designs by C.W. Stephens, architect of much of the Cadogan estate and Harrods department store. The new, seven-storey hotel featured interlinking suites, which meant that up to 15 rooms could be connected on the first, second or third floor, allowing Claridge's to accommodate three heads of state at any one time. The manager of the hotel during the 1920s, Alfred Mambrino, wrote a revealing article, 'Reflection on Atmosphere: The Modern London Hotel', for *Architectural Review*, in which the new, fashionable influence of the Paris exhibition was acknowledged. He explained that when the hotel was built at the end of the Victorian era: '. . . the need of a palace in the heart of Mayfair which would be more than an hotel, a rendezvous of Society in the capital of the Empire' was understood (1927: 130). However, his comments on the changed situation of the 1920s indicate an awareness of a trend towards the feminization of decoration, partly as a result of the 1925 Paris exhibition, at this time when more named women decorators were working professionally: '. . . in a hotel with a social character, it is the woman who matters; the room is then more for the lady who reigns in it. She is the hostess. . . . Society is a lady. All modern decoration in social hotels, as in the public rooms of private houses must thus be a background to her personality' (1927: 132).

Bernard used Lalique glass panels to decorate the side entrance to the restaurant at the Strand Palace Hotel (Figure 12). In the foyer illuminated steps and walls reproduced an effect used in more splendid form at the Alexandre 111 bridge as part of the 1925 exhibition. The theme of the *villes lumières* was a powerful and effective one. 'By night the bridge produced an almost hallucinatory effect: beneath the boutiques with their brightly lit windows seemed to erupt into both the sky and the river – a flood of light flowing through the heart of the city' (Gronberg 1998: 4). The impact of art deco could be seen in the fashionable shopping streets, as well as the luxury hotel districts of London. Small, select fashion shops (Figure 13) served the well-heeled. The building of Selfridge's department store on Oxford Street was American-financed and art deco-inspired, with lift doors designed by Edgar Brandt, reinforcing Parisian style as the leader of fashion in 1925. *Haute-couture* fashion and exclusive interior decoration remained Parisian-dominated in Britain during the 1920s. However, what is fascinating is the way in which the American reinvention of art deco as the new style of glamour and modernity begins to make an impact in Britain.

Figure 12 Strand Palace Hotel, London

The erection of art deco factory buildings in the south of England during the inter-war years came as part of an export drive on the part of American industry and government. The same economic growth that had funded the building of art deco skyscrapers in New York led to the erection of buildings of a similar style, if not a similar scale, in Britain.

As with the film quota system, the British government attempted to stem the American trade invasion by imposing huge tariffs on imported luxury goods. American corporations worked around this by setting up manufacturing plants in Britain – Ford establishing a factory in Dagenham in 1928 and General Motors buying out Vauxhall in 1927. The tyre manufacturers Goodrich, Goodyear and Firestone also avoided the one-third import duties by building new factories in Britain. The Firestone factory built on the Great West Road in 1928 is a prime example of industrial art deco, and significantly reflects American interests in Britain (Figure 14). The factory was designed by the British architectural practice of Wallis, Gilbert and Partners, which had been founded in 1916 to work with Trussed Concrete Steel, an American

Figure 13 Original Art Deco Fashion Illustration

company that specialized in the use of reinforced concrete for factory construction. The commission may have also come via contacts at the Ford Motor Company or followed their successful commission to build the Wrigley's factory at North Wembley (1926–8) (Skinner 1994: 17). The factory was conceived of as an Egyptian tomb, with appropriate Egyptian surface decoration on its façade. For example, the ten stone-faced columns that regularly punctuate the rows of darkened glass have multi-coloured lotus petal capitals. The special, ceremonial causeway and front entrance were only used for prestigious visitors, particularly to act as a backdrop for press coverage of visiting film stars from America. When illuminated at night the façade presented an arresting spectacle, seen from the new, six-lane highway that led from the centre of London to the west. The building was designed to be seen from a speeding car. There was also a link with film here, as Egypt, even before the discovery of Tutankhamun's tomb, had links with magic and sorcery that early cinema had exploited (Lant in Bernstein and Studlar 1997:

Figure 14 Firestone Factory, London

69–98). Theatre buildings would also sometimes echo the Egyptian theme on their façades and interiors, like the Grand Lake Theatre in Oakland, where murals presented an Egyptian desert scene with Tutankhamun's head framed by two golden wings crowning the stage (Stones 1993). Also, the structure of the Firestone factory, with its imposing façade stretching some 200 feet across and shielding the functional factory space extending back about 467 feet, emulated the form of a theatre or cinema with a grand street façade fronting its auditorium. The new building attracted great notoriety at the time and subsequently. The British cultural elite declared it anathema. The modernist architect E. Maxwell Fry thought it an example of '. . . all the worst sentimentalities of uncultured commercialism' when writing on *Design in Modern Life* in 1934 (as quoted in Skinner 1994: 13). The American modernist critic Henry-Russell Hitchcock, in the 1937 Museum of Modern Art exhibition, *Modern Architecture in England*, praised the British public for their taste: 'Yet they make little or no distinction between the most outrageous pseudo-Egyptian factories and the many modern houses shown in this exhibition whose architectural quality would be distinguished anywhere in the world. The British public has proved effectively open-minded in patronizing modern architecture' (1937: 32). American investment in Britain was also visible on the high street, with the Woolworth chain's 350 stores located in most of Britain's cities and towns by 1929. Since everything was priced below sixpence, they undercut the local hardware shops. However, it was Hollywood films that were to mount the biggest challenge to British trade and British values during the late 1920s.

Our Dancing Daughters was released in Britain in January 1929, just after the Firestone Factory was built. The film's reception was similar to that enjoyed on the other side of the Atlantic. Concerns were expressed about the *risqué* depiction of loose morals and modern young women. The British trade paper *Kine Weekly* warned 'Ultra-smart settings, wonderful mounting and dresses, putting over a brisk-moving slice of youthful American over-civilisation, but not for family audiences' (10 January 1929). British cinema managers received pressbooks, just as their American counterparts did, produced by film distributors with ideas for exploitation and publicity.[4] The British pressbook for *Our Dancing Daughters* was particularly aimed at the young, female audience. A full column was occupied by Joan Crawford discussing 'Modern Requirements of Modern Clothes', in which she emphasizes the modernity of her costumes in the film: 'the entire attitude of the present day is expressed in the clothes worn in "Our Dancing Daughters". Activity, speed, flashing movement are the characterizations of the new generation. Clothes invariably reflect the times. They are the mood of the woman.' In a similar vein Anita Page extolled the virtues of matching accessories. *The Bioscope* noted: 'Gorgeous dresses and elaborate appointments of all kinds complete the numerous attractive features of a production which should have a particularly strong appeal for women' (9 January 1929: 57). Joan Crawford's outfits were frequently featured on the pages of *Picturegoer*, Britain's highest-circulation film fan magazine. Selling at one shilling weekly, it featured the latest news of films, actors, actresses and associated gossip and fashion tips. News of Joan Crawford's engagement to Douglas Fairbanks Jr reached the magazine in November 1928, just before the British release of *Our Dancing Daughters*.[5] In the 'Gossips of Hollywood' piece by Reg Mortimer she is pictured in a scanty swimsuit with the caption: 'Until Joan Crawford lately announced her engagement to Douglas Fairbanks jun., rumour gave her no peace' (p. 20). She was featured again in January 1929 in an evening gown designed by David Cox for *Spring Fever* (1927).

It is significant that *Picturegoer* highlights Crawford's defiance of Parisian glamour: 'Devastating and lovely, the gown almost speaks her personality. Unusual in line and treatment, it is of black satin trimmed with silver beads. The skirt falls in several points in front and is higher at the back, a direct contrast to the prevailing "up in front and down behind" movement of Paris' (p. 16). The advertising aimed at female consumers in *Picturegoer* from 1928 to 1930 also encapsulates the shift from Paris to America as the source of glamour. Elegant but dated line drawings are used to advertise some products – La Velouty de Dixor, Paris, *crêpe de chine* underwear sold at Marshall and Snelgrove (Figure 15) and Coty coloured powder in ten shades, which were available in 23 *'Parfums-Créations'*, all with French titles. As a marked contrast, adverts for American goods used the new advertising techniques practised in Britain by J. Walter Thompson, who opened a London office in 1899. New consumer goods such as Persil washing powder were advertised using scantily-clad flappers with declarations of 'Persil is as modern, as up-to-date and different as artificial silk itself' (Figure 16) (December 1928, p. 65). Also, head and shoulder photographs as opposed to line drawings of Hollywood film stars were placed in the adverts to provide endorsements for beauty products, superseding the practice of featuring minor members of the aristocracy or medical experts. Ponds Cold Cream, Ovaltine and Swandown face and Larola face powders were all advertised during the late 1920s using Hollywood stars in *Picturegoer*. Other mass-circulation magazines of the late 1920s also carried adverts that used the endorsements of Hollywood film stars, including *Home Chat*, which featured a photograph of Mary Brian of Universal supporting Lux Toilet Soap and Merna Kennedy, also of Universal, supporting Icilma Vanishing and Cold Creams.

While America had taken the lead as far as glamour was concerned by 1930 for the majority, the architectural profession was less impressed. The growing popularity and social acceptance of film viewing created a problem, in that new cinemas had to be built to accommodate this popular pastime. Moral panic about the conditions of film viewing emerged, as it had in America. The National Council of Public Morals recommended in its report of 1917 that the cinema should be

ORIGINAL LINGERIE

GEORGETTE NIGHTDRESS, square neck, with deep armhole finished with attractive strong coloured lace, flat pleats from shoulder.
Colours: Ivory, pink, peach, coral, lido blue, and green.
Price 35/9
We have also a large selection of original Pyjamas, in crêpe de chine, satin, flowered crêpe de chine, etc.

FASCINATING BACKLESS PINAFORE PETTICOAT in crêpe de chine, satin, triple ninon or georgette trimmed at bust and foot with wide ecru lace, cut all in one piece. A novel feature is the adjustable wrap over back, rendering it suitable for all figures and freedom of movement while maintaining the slim line.
Price 49/6
Attractive Knicker to match with shaped band at waist.
Price 29/6
Colours: Black, ivory, pink, salmon, peach, green, blue, orchid, lemon, etc.

MARSHALL & SNELGROVE
(Debenhams, Ltd.)
VERE STREET & OXFORD STREET, LONDON, W.1
Write for Illustrated Catalogue

Figure 15 Ad from *Picturegoer*

adequately lit to prevent indecent moral conduct. The health scare following the cholera epidemic of 1918 fuelled worries about the spread of germs in theatres. Therefore, film exhibitors attempted to improve the image of visiting the cinema to improve trade. No obvious ideal existed for cinema-building, and so a lively debate over what the ideal cinema should look like animated the pages of the architectural, building and cinema management press during the inter-war years (Paynton 1995). As early as 1915 *The Builder* reprinted an article that had appeared in *American Architect* the previous year. 'American Cinema Theatres' featured Howard Crane's designs for an impressive, two- storey

Figure 16 Persil Advertisement

theatre in Buffalo, New York. The article also recommended the practice of building a spacious foyer to attract and accommodate waiting patrons. Arthur Meoly's *Theatres and Picture Houses* was published in the following year in America, and included detailed advice about erecting this new building type. Heating systems, sight lines and the use of balconies were all discussed and illustrated in this influential volume. The book contained work by Thomas Lamb executed in traditional, French styles.

However, another approach to cinema design was developed in America during the 1920s; known as the atmospheric, it involved constructing a fantasy interior that resembled being outside, in the form of an Italian landscape, an Egyptian desert or a Moroccan village. The ambience of the cinema interior would be further enhanced by the use of fountains, imitation foliage or birds; and a special machine located in the projection booth, the Brenograph, would project the image of floating clouds on to the ceiling to complete the experience.

John Eberson was the pioneer of the atmospheric cinema in America, and his work came to be known in Britain through the professional press. For example, *Ideal Kinema* published an article on 'Atmospherics: Co-ordination between Architect, Artist and Electrician' in 1929. Key examples include the work of Edward Stone, who designed four Astorias in and around London in 1929–30. Two of the cinemas featured Italianate gardens, one an Egyptian desert scene and one a North African village. Stone explained his philosophy in *Ideal Kinema*: '. . . the correct atmosphere for the modern theatre is reached by means of harmonising comfort and restfulness for the body, the simulation of nature to please the eye, and entertainment to provide the antidote to everyday business and everyday home life and worry'. The sub-title for Stone's 1929 piece was 'The Psychology of Atmosphere', revealing the impact of Eberson's American work.

Therefore, the American brand of art deco made some impact in Britain before 1930. The traditional position of Paris as the undisputed leader of taste came to be challenged by America directly through the impact of Hollywood cinema. Designers of cinema buildings, fashion and make-up for the mass market were all looking to America rather than Paris for their lead for the first time in history. The growing impact of a new mass-produced culture to fill leisure time developed in parallel with the growing impact of America in Britain. Hence Americanization becomes linked automatically, and perhaps not all that suprisingly, with mass culture in Britain.

Notes

1. See Bordwell, Staiger and Thompson, *The Classical Hollywood Cinema: Film Style and Mode of Production to 1960* (London: Routledge, 1988).

2. Richard Day had initially worked with Erich von Stronheim since 1919 and the production of *Blind Husband*. During the editing of von Stronheim's

Greed (1925) a merger with MGM took place, and Day started to work for Gibbons. However, according to his son he felt overshadowed by Gibbons, and left in 1930 to work for Samuel Goldwyn.

3. Angela Partington has made a similar point about 1950s British fashion and the democratization of taste and fashionability in her 1992 essay, 'Popular Fashion and Working-Class Affluence' (Ash and Wilson 1992). Importantly, she points out that ideas of what was fashionable and glamorous were reworked and altered by working-class women from Parisian prototypes – it was not a simple matter of Simmel's trickle-down scenario.

4. Pressbooks were generally printed in three sizes; small (11″ × 15″), medium (14″ × 20″) and large (25″ × 19″) in black and white or sepia during the 1920s until the late 1940s, when books appeared in full colour. The BFI in London has a rich collection of such pressbooks, plus souvenir brochures and other important publicity material (Moat 1999).

5. The couple were married on 3 June 1929, just after they had finished filming the sequel to *Our Dancing Daughters*, *Our Modern Maidens*. They were to divorce in 1933, partly as a result of Crawford's torrid affair with Clark Gable.

Bright Style in Dark Days: Streamlined *Moderne* and the Depression

Hollywood glamour was one of the most important aspects of material culture during the inter-war years in America. Whether seen to be something to espouse and aspire to as part of the construction of personal identity or something that threatened core American values or avant-garde practice, it was highly significant. The new phenomenon of visiting the cinema was a popular activity, and the texts surrounding film viewing were consumed avidly as part of the landscape of material culture. For the first time in history America led the rest of the Western world in terms of what was considered glamorous for a mass consumer market. This chapter tracks the changing ideals of glamour in set and film costume design from the streamlined *moderne* of *Grand Hotel* (1932) to the frothy satin and lace of *Camille* (1936). The impact of the *moderne* on architecture, interior decoration, product and fashion design on both sides of the Atlantic is then explored against the backdrop of the Depression years.

White Rooms and Wicked Women

Writing in 1937, Morton Eustis described the mass production techniques that had developed in Hollywood in *Theatre Art Monthly* : 'Thousands of theatres throughout the country have got to be supplied, week in, week out, with tin cans containing reels of celluloid. . . . Production in Hollywood is mass production on a high financial some call it a monopolistic scale. And the miracle of the studios is not that the pictures, the actors, or the sets, are so often bad, but that they are as good as, occasionally, they are' (1937: 785). By 1930 Cedric Gibbons reigned supreme over an industrial-scale art department. The five main

Figure 17 Cedric Gibbons at Work

Hollywood studios – MGM, Warner Brothers, Paramount, 20th Century-Fox and RKO – were run on the corporate model established by Henry Ford for the cheap mass production of cars in the 1900s, which had developed into a functional management structure. The biggest change technically to affect Hollywood during the 1930s was the mass introduction of sound, enabling music, sound effects and recorded dialogue to be incorporated into each film. As the supervising art director at the wealthiest of the five studios, Gibbons would appoint a unit art director to oversee a particular film when it was given the go-ahead from the studio (Figure 17). Sketches for the main sets would be produced and then locations selected and sets built by an army of construction workers. A set decorator would then complete the process by furnishing the sets with objects from shops, whether on loan or purchased outright. In certain cases special props had to be constructed on the lot. As Gibbons explained in 1938: 'It may have been necessary for him (the set dresser) to send abroad for certain pieces, to borrow them from museums, or, in the case of props no longer in existence, or modernistic and imaginative in conception, to have them built in the studio cabinet shop' (Watts 1938: 48). There was also a research department that served to authenticate period drama productions to an astonishingly high level of accuracy. For example, the production of *Marie Antoinette* (1938) entailed an MGM researcher's spending a year in France and taking some 12,000 photographs, from which no fewer than 98 sets were built in Los Angeles to replicate the splendour of Versailles. This was only one film – every year MGM would produce between fifty to sixty features, requiring an average of thirty-five to fifty sets each. Despite the size of the operation, Gibbons had overall control of the look of every film produced by MGM until his retirement in 1956.

The creation of the big white set relied on lighting techniques, and Gibbons supervised the use of brilliant, high-key lighting that created a soft, grey-white, glossy sheen on all the major sets, leaving close-ups to the cinematographer. The older arc lights had necessitated painting anything which should appear white on film in pink or green. The new iridescence was also made possible by the new film stock Changing from orthochromatic to the more sensitive panchromatic meant a far sharper image could be achieved with the use of red filters to achieve the crisper outlines. MGM had always paid attention to the lighting of its pictures, wanting the film image to remain clear whatever the local circumstances of projection. Indeed, this change to the lighting formed part of the publicity for *Our Dancing Daughters* in1928 (Pressbook 1928). The use of key lighting with barely any shadow, and backlighting for close-ups of the stars became a hallmark of MGM films by the early 1930s. One key example is the Oscar-winning *Grand Hotel*, released in 1932 (Figure 18). Set entirely in a luxury hotel in Berlin, the action takes place in the massive lobby, the guest bedrooms and a cocktail bar. The design of the entrance lobby is stunning, with a black and white chequered floor that is cleverly arranged around the central desk in concentric blocks. The lobby forms the ground floor of an atrium, and the entire life of the hotel as a microcosm of life itself is summarized in the bird's-eye establishing shot from the top floor looking straight down past several floors with open balconies to the entrance. This is reinforced by the revolving door by which guests enter. Styled in *moderne* tubular steel and glass and decorated with characteristic horizontal bands, it ushers in the rich and famous as easily as it expels them after their stay. The door is lit from above with round, concealed lights, and the horizontal bands are echoed within the lobby. The film

Figure 18 Still from *Grand Hotel*

also acts as a microcosm of modernity in its use of telephones. A huge novelty in the 1930s, telephones in hotel rooms were the height of luxury. The plot is interconnected by means of the telephone, and the impoverished baron (John Barrymore) is even murdered by being struck with a telephone receiver. The film cuts intermittently to the telephone switchboard, where lines of women wear identical headsets and almost become part of the machinery of the switchboard.

The sense of luxury and modernity is accentuated by integrating the lead women of the film into their settings through the use of clothing. The bedroom of Greta Garbo, playing a rather bored Russian ballerina, is adorned with shimmering cream satin on the walls, the chair and the bed, and this same material is used for her pyjamas.[1] A prominent dressing-table is featured in the bedroom, with oval mirror and elegantly curved drawers and central support. Garbo is dressed by Adrian in a floor-length gown with full, diaphanous sleeves in her hotel room, and swathes herself in a fur-collared coat when she ventures outside.

Joan Crawford, playing a fortune-seeking stenographer, is sleeker than in the 'Our' series, with longline dresses by Adrian, influenced by the bias-cut designs of couturiers in Paris like Madeleine Vionnet or Worth. The cloche hat was now out of fashion, and so hair could be grown slightly longer, away from the boyish schoolboy bobs of the 1920s. Crawford has longer, straightened hair, heavy eyeliner and accentuated lips. Adrian's design for one of Crawford's dresses featured in the film has four buttons arranged in pairs and offset collar – the openness and immodesty of the collar suggesting Crawford's availability to men in the film (Gaines and Herzog 1990: 193).

The big white set was used in the majority of MGM films that dealt with contemporary themes during the 1930s, before the widespread adoption of filming in colour negated its importance in the 1950s. Key examples include Joan Crawford's *Possessed* (1931), *When Ladies Meet* (1933) and *Private Lives* (1934). In *Dinner at Eight* (1933) Jean Harlow, with her platinum hair and all-white, dazzling gown, complete with 22-inch white ostrich feathers decorating the sleeves, shimmers in a set composed of eleven shades of white by Gibbons and Hobart Erwin (Figure 19). However, it is important to bear in mind that these sets made a crucial contribution to the narrative. In *Dinner at Eight* the all-white room is the setting for Harlow and her loathsome, *nouveau-riche* husband, played by Wallace Beery. The dressing-table denotes luxury and glamour, with three tiers of deep cream fringing, also used to decorate the matching stool. Reflective surfaces feature not only in the three mirrors but also in the main surface of the table, which is of

Figure 19 Still from *Dinner at Eight*

glass and is strewn with various glass bottles containing cosmetics, perfumes and oils. The lush decoration of the dressing-table is further enhanced by the four pairs of white plumes that crown each corner of the mirrors. The thick, luxurious floor covering and the all-pervasive drapes also contribute to the atmosphere of almost claustrophobic glamour. Here the glittering *moderne* setting seems to suggest the superficiality of *arriviste* taste, manners and morals. In complete contrast, the remainder of the action takes place in the more conventional classical revival surroundings of their upper-class friends. Harlow provides a stark contrast in the dark, 'tasteful' surroundings by wearing a full-length white fitted satin dress with plunging back accessorized by long white gloves, numerous jewelled bracelets and white fur stole.

In MGM musicals, such as *Broadway Melody of 1936,* lavish dance numbers take place against a mock Manhattan skyline at night with *moderne* surroundings. However, the newspaper office, theatre and producer's office lack any hint of glamour or high style. By the time of the release of *Broadway Melody of 1936*, Hollywood was transforming itself into a more family-based, morally centred organization. In design terms this led to a softening of the sets. For example, in *Camille* (1936) Greta Garbo is seen draped across satin-covered beds; but the pillows are trimmed with lace, and her gown is decorated with sequins. There are flounced curtains at the windows and quilted, upholstered chairs. Even on final frame of the main film the words 'The End' are superimposed against a satin pillow edged with lace. This starkly contrasts the brittle amorality of her status as a fallen woman with her former mobility, which underlies her character and, above all, her femininity, redeemed by her death at the end. The values the film espoused, partly owing to the impact of the Hays Code, were those of middle America (Sklar 1994). And so, ten years after contributing to the success of the lusty 'Our' series, Cedric Gibbons was to be found concentrating on the fantasy designs for *The Wizard of Oz* (1939).

Gibbons was the most important of the art directors, introducing art deco, the *moderne* and the big white set to Hollywood. However, the creations of Van Nest Polgese at RKO were also significant, and again used set design to represent narrative intent. The Astaire–Rogers musicals with unit art director Carroll Clark, including *Top Hat* (1935), use this device. The film begins with Fred Astaire awaiting his producer friend in a stuffy London gentlemen's club. The décor is heavy and almost Edwardian, with exaggerated chandeliers and winged, upright chairs. Astaire cocks a snook at the assembled gentlemen when he leaves, breaking into a tap dance that pierces the suffocating club rule of silence in the smoking room. The familiar backdrop for the examination of social climbing, the luxury hotel, is employed once again in the film with *moderne* settings. A key moment is when Ginger Rogers is awakened in her white bed, with its satin quilt, sheets, and pyjamas and luxurious quilted, semi-circular back (Figure 20). As she sleeps in

Figure 20 Still from *Top Hat*

the room beneath Astaire and his friend, it is Astaire's tap-dancing feet that arouse her from her slumber. As was common with all Hollywood films of the 1930s, particularly following the adoption of the Hays Code in 1930, a woman's bed could not be openly shown when a man was in the room. Hence, many beds in bedroom shots are raised on a plinth; or, as in the case of *Top Hat*, a modest, diaphanous veil is draped across an archway when a male is shown in the room with Ginger present. The bed takes on a further symbolic quality later in the narrative when Astaire discovers Rogers's marriage to another, and enters the suite in the hotel where she is destined to spend her honeymoon. Astaire lounges on the same bed, declaring to Rogers's new husband that he has the key to the suite, hinting that he has the key to Rogers's heart. The actors, narrative and sets combine to create the spectacle of the film itself. No one aspect can be separated out from the total experience. *Top Hat* also featured the an extravagant recreation of Venice with three oversized, Baroque curved bridges and water dyed black to create the appropriate contrasts.

Enforcing a Moral Code

By 1930 a different set of rules governed the look of Hollywood film sets, for a wide variety of economic, political and cultural reasons. From October 1929 the Stock Market Crash deeply affected all aspects of American commercial life: the era of conspicuous consumption and art deco extravagance was over. The film industry itself was maturing and, in an attempt to assuage middle-class critics, a Production Code was agreed in 1930 by the industry, particularly to control the excesses of the 'gold digger' and 'fallen woman' pictures. In *Our Blushing Brides* (1929), Crawford plays an honest and hard-working shop assistant rather than the rich and idle party-girl of previous years. It is interesting to note that the chief motivation behind the introduction of the Production Code was the perceived need for the cultural elite to safeguard standards. As Balio has observed: 'An increasingly insecure Protestant provincial middle class sought to defend its cultural hegemony from the incursions of a modernist, metropolitan culture that the provincials regarded as alien – a word that was often, but not always, a synonym for Jewish' (1990: 45). An extract from the Code itself reveals this concern for the influence of a mass culture on the population:

> Most arts appeal to the mature. This art appeals at once to every class, mature, immature, developed, underdeveloped, law abiding, criminal. Music has its grades for different classes; so has literature and drama. This art of the motion picture, combining as its does the two fundamental appeals of looking at a picture and listening to a story, at once reached [*sic*] every class of society. [Thus] it is difficult to produce films intended for only certain classes of people. . . . Films, unlike books and music, can with difficulty be confined to certain selected groups (as quoted in Jacobs 1995: 10).

The guardians of moral values were also extending their remit at this time beyond alcohol – Prohibition ran from 1919 to 1933 – to women's dress. The flapper dresses worn by Anita Page and Joan Crawford, which many young women admired, were outrageously short for the time, and legislation was introduced to prevent such garments being worn in public. For example, in Utah a Bill was introduced: '. . . providing fine and imprisonment for those who wore on the streets "skirts higher than three inches above the ankle"; and a Bill introduced in the Ohio legislature sought to prohibit any "female over fourteen years of age" from wearing "a skirt which does not reach that part of the foot known as the instep"' (Laver 1969: 232). Hence, the decision of the motion picture industry to introduce a Production Code was taken at a time when restrictions on the new and the modern in other aspects of popular culture were in evidence.

According to the Code it was no longer acceptable to show sex being explicitly exchanged for glamorous, luxury belongings. Lea Jacobs's thorough review of the MPPDA censorship files reveals moral outrage on the part of women's and religious interest groups about this category of film. This also informed popular journalism on the subject, which construed the label of glamour as morally, ethically or intellectually suspect – for example, *Photoplay*: 'Charm? No! No! You Must Have Glamour' (Jacobs 1995: 16). But the use of contemporary style in set design and costume remained an important indicator of the immoral woman. As Jacobs has observed:

> By the thirties, the association between the fallen woman and art *moderne* was so well established that it was exploited as a part of a film's advertising campaign. The press kit for *The Greeks Had a Word for Them* advised exhibitors to decorate their lobbies in a 'modernistic' black and silver color scheme: 'Since most of the scenes photographed in the picture show modernistic furnishings in the apartment of the gold diggers, it is therefore in keeping with the general theme of the picture' (1995: 55).

Because of the pressures of the Production Code, the film's original title of *The Greeks Had a Word For It* had to be changed. The thirty outfits for the three leading actresses in *The Greeks Had a Word For Them* were designed by Coco Chanel. The top French couturière was brought over from Paris by Samuel Goldwyn in 1931 to work on the film about three New York social climbers. The total cost of the outfits was over $100,000 US and an entire department was set up for Chanel on the MGM lot. However, Chanel soon returned to Paris, disenchanted with the work of designing for film.

Evenings of Luxury

In Britain, cinema attendance during the 1930s continued to show a dramatic increase, particularly after the introduction of the 'talkies'. Total cinema attendance for the whole of 1934 was 903 million, reaching 946 million in 1937 and 990 million by 1939 (Browning and Sorrell 1954: 134). The average number of visits to the cinema was two per week; it was a significant part of life, particularly for children and young adults (Rowson 1939; Kuhn 1997). This was enhanced by an explosion in cinema building during the 1930s, so that by 1940 there were 5,500 cinemas in Britain, and every town had at least one. The pennygaffs were superseded by the flea-pits in working-class areas; but cinema building in the new suburbs succeeded in appealing to the middle class and particularly to women for daytime use, to view a matinée with friends or children or use the comparatively lavish restaurant and café facilities. The hygiene of the new cinemas was emphasized in advertising, with ventilation systems, rubber flooring for the foyer and foam seating providing a clean and germ-free environment. But it was the luxury and glamour of the cinema surroundings that the audience valued at the time. In a recent survey by Annette Kuhn, *Cinema Culture in 1930s Britain,* over 90 per cent of her respondents used words such as 'comfort, space, luxury, modernity' to describe their memories of going to the pictures (1997a,b). Cinema designers and managers were well aware of the need to create a feeling of luxury and quality. In *The Kinematograph Yearbook* (1934) cinema managers were advised: 'The question of floor covering has also to be considered. In the auditorium carpeting affords that de-luxe atmosphere so essential to patron good will' (p. 34). Cinema design was heavily American-inspired; the atmospheric cinema ceased to hold an appeal with the introduction of the talkies. The Hollywood film company Paramount had opened two luxury cinemas in London – the Plaza and the Carlton – in 1926-7. This was followed by a small chain of luxury cinemas in major British cities to preview their films, including the early Marx Brothers comedies. The architectural firm of Verity and Beverley were responsible for these transatlantic super-cinemas, which would seat as many as 4,000.

The Paramount in Manchester opened in 1930, and was the only British cinema at that time to boast an American-style mezzanine balcony between the stalls and the main balcony. The Paramount in Newcastle opened in the following year, with the same seating arrangement. The auditorium was decorated with sixteen Watteau-style, hand-painted panels, which were 35 feet high. The huge foyer had an art deco balustrade made from aluminium alloy, art deco mirrors, side tables and plush carpeting. This was a truly impressive cinema to visit. The first time my mother went to the cinema it was to see Walt Disney's first feature-length animated film *Snow White and the Seven Dwarfs* (1937) during the war – the film that Kuhn's survey also found to be the most frequently recalled film of the 1930s (Kuhn 1997a). My mother lived in Lobley Hill, and recalled: 'It was a big treat to go to the cinema in Newcastle. The cinema had a big wide staircase with thick carpet and everything was gilt' (Interview with author 1998). As one of Jackie Stacey's respondents recalled: 'Our favourite cinema was the Ritz – with its deep pile carpet and double weeping staircase coming down one always felt like a heroine descending into a ballroom' (1994: 194). The Paramount in Newcastle became part of the Odeon chain in 1937, and I remember going to see *The Sound of Music* there in 1965 and feeling like a princess as I walked down the staircase, out of the lavish doors into the chilly north-eastern night. Imagine what it felt like during the Depression! There was a boom in cinema construction during 1932–4 as more, larger, purpose-built venues were erected to accommodate the technology required for sound. As Nicholas Hiley has noted: 'By 1934, some 1.8 million of the country's 3.9 million seats were in cinemas capable of holding more than 1000' (1999: 43). From 1934 until the outbreak of the Second World War a further 350,000 extra seats were created in new or refurbished cinemas, matched by a 10 per cent increase in attendance.

In Britain the 1927 Cinematograph Films Act remained in force until it was renewed in a second act in 1938. Although there were trade restrictions in place to encourage the British film industry, they did not yield the desired results. The only successful British production of the 1930s in financial and critical terms was *The Private Life of Henry V111* (1933). Directed by Alexander Korda and produced by London Film Productions, it showed an impressive return of £500,000 on its first world run, which included showing in a selection of American cities (Jarvie 1992: 144). However, this pattern of distribution was difficult for British companies to emulate, as London Film Productions had a special link with United Artists, enabling distribution in America. The popularity of Hollywood film amongst the working and lower-middle classes was completely overwhelming. The main impact of the 1927 Act was to create an industry for 'quota quickies', whereby American renters were compelled to show British films and therefore commissioned cheaply-made, substandard films that could not compete with their well-financed American counterparts.

Britain clung, ineffectively, to the imposition of quotas, while seeking to encourage more collaboration between the two countries in terms of joint financing of projects. As Peter Stead has acutely observed, there is a consistent pattern in British attitudes to film:

A national film institute, a network of film societies, a number of intellectual film journals, a whole tradition of documentary film-making and close links between those interested in film and educationalists, especially those engaged in adult education . . . One is always struck by the optimism; the break-through was always just around the corner and any day the masses would opt for quality films (Stead 1989: 27).

Jarvie has convincingly argued that the British intellectual and political elites feared Hollywood films: 'Obstinately, however, the masses preferred Hollywood films, films that some intellectuals feared would teach ordinary British people a different (and classless) language, make them less respectful, less religious, more footloose and ambitious, and less law-abiding' (1992: 152). The masses might also be less interested in adult education too! While the British elite equated Americanization with social mobility, viewed in a negative sense, and regarded Hollywood dominance as a major factor in this process, in America too the supposedly damaging influences of film on morality, behaviour and national values were debated, and informed policy-making.

By 1933 the American film industry was at a low ebb, financially insecure and perceived by the WASP elite as morally bankrupt. The industry looked to a strengthening of the Production Code under William Hays to reassure the public and the use of more acceptable story lines to reassure the moral majority, particularly after the alarmist publication of the Payne Fund Studies in 1933. This five-year research programme had investigated the effects of Hollywood film on young people and come to some alarming conclusions about a decline in moral standards. In design terms, film was made more respectable through the creation of the big white set and use of the *moderne* style as a more acceptable alternative to the morally corrupt art deco. *Moderne*, through the growth in consumerism in the 1930s and the linking of a contemporary style to the fortunes of America, lost its decadent, Parisian overtones. It may also have been that all forms of modernity in design were becoming more acceptable, and could be seen to signal wealth legitimately earned or inherited, as opposed to ill-gotten. The films were now less *risqué*, with more family-orientated plots and stars, and the cinemas themselves were also made far more attractive and respectable in the 1930s, particularly to attract the middle-class female audience and perhaps their children.

Consumption and Copying the Movies

The set designs and clothes were part of the material culture of the time, and drew upon the same values and concerns as other aspects of consumption. The audience could also reinforce the experience by emulating the stars, clothes and sets they admired and taking the film outside the cinema in the process of consumption.

As Blumer had proved in his contribution to the Payne Studies in the late 1920s, films did inform or mirror the audience's tastes and preferences in terms of fashion and mannerisms. This link was to be fully exploited by the Hollywood studios, who worked closely with retailers in what are now known as 'tie-ins'. This was particularly the case for films exploiting the art deco or *moderne* styles, as it was perceived that the look of the film would appeal to the female consumer. *Our Dancing Daughters* is a case in point, with *The Bioscope* noting in its review: 'Gorgeous dresses and elaborate appointments of all kinds complete the numerous attractive features of a production which should have a particularly strong appeal for women' (BFI, Pressbook 1929: 57). And the appeal was exploited quite literally by the studios in the 'Exploitation' pages of the Press Books, which gave the exhibitors ideas for displays at the cinemas, newspaper or magazine advertising and shops. A Cinema Shop was established at the New York department store Macy's where imitations of the clothes worn by the female stars in recent films could be bought. Jane Gaines has researched the Greta Garbo, MGM film *Queen Christina* (1933), and found: '. . . suits, coats, and hostess gowns (but not trousers) "inspired" by the film were offered for sale at the Cinema Shop along with a special promotion of half-price tableware' (Gaines 1989: 49–50).

The most famous example is that of the dress worn by Joan Crawford in *Letty Lynton* (1932). Designed by Adrian in white starched chiffon, it was widely copied by the New York fashion industry. This was apparently encouraged by the studio's leaking details of the gown in advance of the release of the film. Macy's reputedly sold 50,000 cheap copies of the dress; however, as Gaines and Herzog have argued, there is no empirical proof for this figure. Mass-produced copies of the dress certainly did exist, as one was included in the Smithsonian Institute's 'Hollywood: Legend and Reality' travelling exhibition of 1986 (Gaines and Herzog 1990: 88) What is clear from an examination of publicity sources is that copies of outfits worn in films were mass-produced for fashion retailers. It is clear that sewing and knitting patterns were also produced to imitate the clothes seen on the screen, enabling any working-class or lower-middle-class woman to emulate her favourite clothes. As Gaines and Herzog argue, this was not a matter of simple, passive imitation in the hypodermic popular culture model espoused by the Frankfurt School:

> Following a straight mass culture manipulation theory, one would argue that the function of all motion picture fashion information, whether it appeared in advice columns or advertisements, was to persuade women to buy clothes and cosmetics instead of devising homemade beauty ornaments and treatments. We have found in the material surveyed here, however, a respect for the fashion practices and preferences of ordinary women (1990: 87).

There was a carefully considered matching of personal identity and style with the choices available, a process more akin to the of objectification–subjectification model proposed by Daniel Miller (1987).

As Jackie Stacey found in her survey of female fans during the 1940s and 1950s, the activity of being a fan is a complex and individual one: 'Copying is the most common form of identificatory practice outside the cinema. Perhaps this is not surprising given the centrality of physical appearance to femininity in general in this culture, and to female Hollywood stars in particular' (1994: 155). Stacey further argues that this is made possible through the process of consumption. Women could not only buy or make an adapted copy of the favoured clothing worn by film stars, they could alter their hairstyles to match the stars or purchase make-up in an effort to present a glamorous image. As Simmel argued, in the age of modernity consumers select particular fashions to express at once a sense of belonging but also a sense of distinction and differentiation (Frisby and Featherstone 1997: 189). Classical Hollywood cinema is a prime example of the process, whereby a range of female stars present an array of possible styles within certain limits. The consumer is active in the sophisticated selection of which star(s) to emulate and how.

The simplistic Frankfurt School model of mass culture also does not apply to the design process itself. The leading Hollywood dress designer, Adrian, needed to second-guess design trends in his work. As he stated in 1938: 'With modern fashions, I get entirely away from current trends, for screen fashions must, of necessity, be designed so that they will be, dramatically, months ahead when they will be seen on the screen by the world at large' (As quoted in Gaines and Herzog 1990: 55). Therefore, Hollywood needed to be as aware of coming trends as designers and buyers in New York, London and Paris. The production studios did not simply pick an image and sell it unproblematically. The image needed to be fashionable and current. The link between fashion, film and consumption is far more complex.

Part of the complexity lies in the way in which Hollywood cinema created and then legitimated make-up for women from the process of filming itself. Indeed, make-up was not really worn by respectable women before the 1930s. It was neither socially acceptable nor widely available. However, the advent of the film industry had necessitated a different approach to make-up as it had been developed for the stage. Theatrical greasepaint tended to dry to form a tough mask that cracked when the actor's face moved – this was not a problem on stage, where hairline cracks were not visible, but proved inadequate for film work. It was Max Factor who introduced film make-up by creating a pancake cream as opposed to stick, which the actors in early film used enthusiastically, as it allowed them more freedom of facial expression. He founded his Hollywood empire on his early involvement with the film industry. With the introduction of panchromatic film in the later 1920s more intensive lighting had to be introduced, as the sputtering of the arc lights was picked up by the new, more sensitive microphones. The new tungsten lighting was more intense, but also allowed for great definition of detail. Max Factor produced a new set of film make-up that would deal with the problem. He also launched his 'Society Make Up' in the late 1920s to a wider audience, beyond the cinema screen (Figure 21). The word 'Cosmetics' was much more usual for everyday wear at that time; but Max Factor introduced the more theatrical and filmic term 'make-up', forging the link between his products and Hollywood glamour that was to prove so successful. In 1928 Max Factor opened a new showroom and studio in Los Angeles. The marketing of his Society Make-Up range was orchestrated through advertising and drug store window displays that built on the endorsements of stars like Joan Crawford – one drugstore display of 1929 actually featured a cut-out of Crawford with a signed letter of endorsement, building on the nineteenth-century practice of doctors' recommending medicine in advertising. In the press book for *Our Blushing Brides* a full window display was offered by Max Factor featuring production shots of Crawford and Anita Page and the full co-operation of Max Factor representatives. Beyond these 'tie-ins' and film imitations, Hollywood cinema played a crucial role in creating and disseminating a streamlined *moderne* style that made a massive impact internationally.

Figure 21 Max Factor Advertisement

Moderne, Transience and Shopping in America

Based on the inspiration of streamlining, the *moderne* style was sleeker and simpler than art deco. The style combined the art deco chic of the 1920s with new, industrial streamlining techniques, giving rise to smooth, sheer surfaces that disguised the inner workings of new technological gadgets. The rounded edges and sweeping curves of the *moderne* could also be interpreted as offering a unity to a diverse American society. It projected a vision of the future that was egalitarian and democratic in a present that was still divided in terms of class, race and gender. This took place at the same time as Hollywood made the effort, through the Production Code in 1930, to appeal to a broader audience and refute middle-class criticisms about the corrupting influence of cinema. So the *moderne* style lacked the amoral connotations of continental, hedonistic art deco. It offered reassurance during the Depression, when society became increasingly fragmented and insecure. It relied on industrial mass production for the manufacture of new consumer products for the home and for their look. It exploited new materials like bakelite, vitrolite, polished aluminium and stainless steel, as well as new techniques for manufacturing more complex, streamlined shapes for cars and trains. It also drew on the new, positive image of science. At America's own international fair, the Century of

Figure 22 Museum of Modern Art Exhibition – Machine Art

Progress Exposition of 1933, the official themes were: 'Science Finds – Industry Applies – Man Conforms.'

Taking some aspects of art deco, the *moderne* also combined aspects of pure International Style, then also beginning to make an impact in America, largely through the activities of the Museum of Modern Art in New York. In architecture, this style was epitomized by the work of Le Corbusier and Walter Gropius in Europe from the mid-1920s onwards. It was characterized by flat roofs, ribbon windows and white rendered exteriors with open plan interiors. Commissioned only by wealthy individuals or public authorities before the Second World War, it was both avant-garde and elitist (Figure 22). Alfred Barr, the first Director of the Museum of Modern Art, was an apostle of the International Style in architecture and European Modernism in general. Exhibitions at MOMA from his appointment in 1927 celebrated,

explained and justified the predominantly French and German achieve-
ments of International Style architects. Barr and his modernist supporters,
including the architect Philip Johnson, had little regard for the adoption
of art deco in America or for the development of the *moderne*. Writing
in the Preface to the publication that accompanied the 1931 exhibition
of the International Style exhibition Barr discussed the book, *Poets of
Steel*. He argued:

> *Poets of Steel*, a characteristic essay on modern American architecture, is
> as one might expect primarily concerned with skyscrapers, although one
> of Mr. Cram's churches is illustrated and Frank Lloyd Wright is mentioned
> only to be dismissed as a mere theorist. But skyscrapers are accepted as
> 'one of the most magnificent developments of our times' – Romanesque,
> Mayan, Assyrian, Renaissance, Aztec, Gothic, and especially Modernistic
> – everything from the stainless steel gargoyles of the Chrysler building
> to the fantastic mooring mast atop the Empire State. No wonder that
> some of us who have been appalled by this chaos turn with the utmost
> interest and expectancy to the International Style (1966: 12–13).

What supporters of avant-garde, International Style design advocated
was a timeless aesthetic, whereby a building would be erected or a chair
manufactured that would never by considered out of fashion. This belief
contradicted mainstream, commercial American designers and manufacturers, who deliberately created built-in obsolescence and revelled
in a plurality of attractive, decorative styles.

Ernest Elmo Calkins was one of the most important figures in the
American advertising world and one of the driving forces behind the
trend of stylistic obsolescence (Heller 1995). He founded the Calkins
and Holden advertising agency in 1903, and was an enthusiastic
supporter of the new advertising profession and one of the founder
members of the Art Directors Club of New York, with its important
round of annual exhibitions, in 1920. Calkins, like many advertising
and marketing practitioners, visited the Paris exhibition in 1925 and
brought back the excitement of a refreshingly new style in art to New
York. By 1930 he was extolling the virtues of using new styles in terms
of obsolescence. Writing in *Modern Publicity* he stated: 'The styling of
manufactured goods is a by-product of improved advertising design
. . . The technical term for this idea is obsoletism. We no longer wait
for things to wear out. We displace them with others that are not more
efficent but more attractive' (as quoted in Heller 1995: 60–3) (Figure
23). Hence, purveyors of the *moderne* style lacked the philosophical

Figure 23 *Moderne* Advertisement

and political reforming motivation of the International Style. They were consciously adopting a style that would suit the purposes of selling products to the middle classes and were quite content to revise or replace the given style as consumer tastes changed. The style was deliberately sold as being American. It was supported by the propaganda of the 1933 Chicago Century of Progress Exposition, the 1939 New York World's Fair and the San Francisco Golden Gate Exhibition. The International Style differed in that its practitioners, who were mainly European architects, argued that theirs was not a style in the sense of a contingent surface or superficial look but a logical, holistic and inevitable set of solutions to functional problems, necessarily conforming to the precepts of 'truth to materials' and 'form follows function'. The misguided public only needed to be educated into appreciating the International Style: hence the reason for founding MOMA in New York. However, the rhetoric and ideological programme of modernism did not enjoy mass appeal, and the post-depression economic recovery took place sheathed in the *moderne* style or 'period' decoration.

Less decorative than art deco, it lent itself to a more economical and thrifty era. Shop fronts or cafés were refitted in the *moderne* style without the necessity of a complete rebuilding. Founded on optimism for the future, embodied in the Roosevelt regime, which began in 1933, and the Works Progress Administration (WPA), the *moderne* was simple, swept back and stylish. David Gebhard has argued that part of the inspiration for the style came from science-fiction (1996: 13). Indeed, the leading science-fiction magazine of the period, *Amazing Stories*, first appeared in 1925, and *Science Wonder Stories* in 1929, the same year as the comic-strip 'Buck Rogers of the 25th Century' was launched. The general preoccupation with speed and transportation at this time also contributed toward the creation of the style. Mass-produced cars, aeroplanes and bullet-shaped trains were an important part of material culture and everyday experience. They also featured heavily in Hollywood films of the 1930s – ships in *Transatlantic* (1931), *Transatlantic Merry Go Round* (1934), *Dodsworth* (1936), *Follow The Fleet* (1935) and *Shall We Dance* (1937); streamlined trains in *Sweet Music* (1935) and *Broadway Melody of 1936* (1935); and aeroplanes in *Top Hat* (1935) and *Flying Down to Rio* (1933). The largely symbolic benefits of streamlining were extolled in popular magazines such as *Esquire, Scientific American* and *Popular Mechanics* during the 1930s. By 1937 all mass-produced cars made in America were streamlined (Gebhard 1996).

One of the major inspirations for streamlining came from air travel. Lindbergh's transatlantic flight of 1927 had attracted national interest, as had the possibility of air travel for all. The new aeroplanes designed from 1929 onwards were smooth and streamlined, unlike the more basic geometric forms of earlier in the century. The Lockheed Sirius of 1929 and the Douglas DC-1, 2 and 3 of 1931–5 encapsulated the streamlined look. A rear view of the *DC-3* appeared as the frontispiece of Sheldon and Martha Cheney's *Art and the Machine* in 1936 with the caption: 'Sources of idioms of machine-age art; streamline, long hard edge, sheer surface, and repetition of simple motives as seen in an airplane' (1936: iv). Norman Bel Geddes promoted streamlining in his 1932 book *Horizons*, as it created the impression of efficiency and speed. Bel Geddes designed the interior of the Pan American Airways flying boat, *China Clipper*, in 1934. The design featured upholstered seating and wall coverings that could be unzipped for cleaning or inspection. This flying boat starred in a Warner Brothers film of the same name in 1936 alongside Pat O'Brien and Humphrey Bogart. The *China Clipper* was one of three built for Pan American Airways, and became synonymous with glamorous travel and exotic destinations, having a range of 2,400 to 3,000 miles across the Pacific.

The group of professionals who contributed most to the creation of the *moderne* and ensured its permeation into many aspects of America life were the industrial designers. Treat as creative geniuses in early design history and then dismissed by later material culture studies, I would argue that industrial designers play an important part in the general discourse of consumption as it was played out during the 1930s in America. Daniel Miller has argued that design history: 'As conventionally studied, . . . is clearly intended to be a form of pseudo art history, in which the task is to locate great individuals such as Raymond Loewy or Norman Bel Geddes and portray them as the creators of modern mass culture' (Miller 1987: 142). He goes on to claim that the links between the designers and industry are perfectly clear and have been argued through in the pages of *Block* and by Adrian Forty (1986); but they have still neglected: 'the transformation of goods in consumption' (Miller 1987: 142). My purpose in raising the issue of designers in the creation of a specific consumer culture during the 1930s in America is to consider their contribution to the consumption of goods. A particular image of the designer was constructed as part of the culture of modernity during this period. Through the pages of the business magazine *Fortune* they were heralded as the visionaries who were reshaping American consumer goods. An article that appeared in *Fortune* February 1934 entitled 'Both Fish and Fowl' chronicled the massive increases in sales stimulated by redesigning consumer goods. In mass-circulation home magazines like *House Beautiful* the designers' own apartments were featured. For example, in January 1939, Walter Dorwin Teague was described as 'designer to millions', underlining the role of the designer in mass-produced goods. Significantly he is also celebrated as 'a man of great taste, quiet and distinguished and assured' (*House Beautiful* 1939: 19). Hence, American mass consumption and its reputed architects – the designers – acquired some of the prestige of and displaced the supremacy earlier enjoyed by European high culture and design and its artists, which had dominated the earlier part of the century. Design was no longer the exclusive domain of the wealthy elite who inherited good taste; design and 'taste' could now be provided for millions by American industrial designers.

The new image of modernity was appropriated by designers in their repackaging of consumer goods (Smith 1993). The design careers of Norman Bel Geddes, Henry Dreyfuss and Raymond Loewy are useful in terms of chronicling this repackaging of mass-produced, consumer objects. For example, the urbane Loewy set up his design consultancy in 1929 after leaving his native France to join his brother in New York

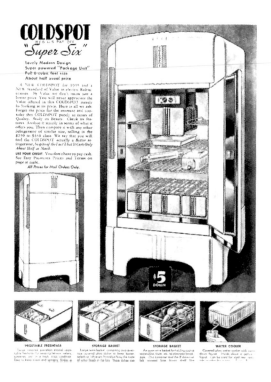

Figure 24 Sears Roebuck Coldspot Icebox

in 1919. He worked chiefly as a fashion illustrator during the 1920s, but in 1929 he undertook his first design work for the British-based manufacturer, Sigmund Gestetner. Gestetner asked Loewy to improve the design of his firm's duplicating machine within three days. Loewy's approach was typical of this first generation of industrial designers: he basically enclosed the workings of the machine in a smooth casing, in this instance made from wood. The machine was transformed into an acceptable piece of smart office furniture, with the dangerous and dirty mechanisms screened. Loewy then applied the same principle to the Coldspot Icebox, which he redesigned for Sears Roebuck in 1937 (Figure 24). The sharp corners and supporting feet were totally enclosed in smooth, white enamelled metal. Loewy emphasized horizontal lines, with elongated handle and chrome at the base of the fridge, housing a storage drawer. Sears Roebuck were, according to Loewy, delighted with the new design, which doubled sales during the first year of production. Loewy was retained by Sears to restyle the fridge twice more to stimulate sales.

Figure 25 Raymond Loewy, Greyhound Bus

From this success Loewy launched his glittering design career: his consultancy grew into an international organization, with offices in New York, London and Paris and with clients including Coca-Cola, the Greyhound Corporation and Studebaker. Loewy restyled the boxy Greyhound buses into the familiar teardrop shape, with horizontal strips impressed down the sides of the vehicle to symbolize speed (Figure 25). Loewy was the most publicity-aware of the new generation of designers, enjoying photo-opportunities and promoting himself. In 1934 he designed a model office with Lee Simonson for the exhibition *Contemporary American Industrial Art* at the Metropolitan Museum of Art, in which he posed imperiously for photographs (Figure 26). Again, the edges of the room are sheathed in a smooth, streamlined form – this time made from white Formica – with horizontal metal bands running round the room, blue linoleum on the floor, recessed lighting and blueprints for a boat on the walls. The overall effect was one of sleek efficiency and control; there was no decoration or clutter. A model for an early car, designed by Loewy, the Hupomobile, had pride of place on a tubular steel plinth.

Teague, like Loewy, began his career in design as a freelance illustrator, working mainly for advertising agencies. After a visit to Paris in 1925 he returned to New York to found his industrial design consultancy. His first major project was for Eastman Kodak, when he designed the

Figure 26 Raymond Loewy, Exhibition at Metropolitan Museum of Art, New York, 1934

Bantam special camera in 1928. This launched a lifelong partnership between Kodak and Teague, with Teague designing a new version of the Kodak Bantam Special in 1936 with the now familiar chrome horizontal strips. In common with his design contemporaries he also published his autobiography- come-design manual, *Design This Day: The Technique of Order in the Machine Age*, in 1940.

Architecture in the *moderne* style was less prevalent than in advertising or the restyling of products. Whilst new building required a major capital investment, repackaging did not. There are fewer examples of building in the *moderne* style in New York than of the boomtime deco of the 1920s. For example the Radio City Music Hall, built as part of the Rockefeller Centre complex and designed by Raymond Hood with interior by Donald Deskey in 1931, displays a transition from art deco to a sleeker, streamlined appearance. The exterior canopy is *moderne* in its use of curved corners, twin horizontal bands and illuminated lettering. Inside, the effect of imposing glamour in the lobby is partly achieved through the use of floor-to-ceiling mirrors and scarlet patterned plush carpets designed by Ruth Reeves. Modernity was connoted in the furniture and lighting fixtures, made from tubular and cast aluminium. Transport in the form of ocean liners inspired the design of the Ladies' Lounge. The Auditorium was built to seat a mass audience of 6,200. The concentric arched ceiling of this massive, hemispherical space ensured perfect acoustics for the mixture of stage performance and sound films that the theatre showed.

This form of auditorium had already been used in the construction of the first, purpose-built cinema to show 'talkies', the Avalon Theatre in the Casino complex on Santa Catalina Island, California, built in 1929, which the Radio City engineers had visited. Also designed by Hood is the McGraw-Hill Building, an apartment block of 1931. The horizontal is emphasized by means of the fenestration and the alternating broad bands in metal and blue-green tile that decorate the main façade. However, much of the important development in New York had taken place before the Wall Street crash. It was not until the more prosperous 1950s that wholesale building began again. In Los Angeles the situation was different, in that the film industry remained comparatively solvent. The Municipal Ferry Building of 1939, now the Los Angeles Maritime Museum, and the Pan Pacific Auditorium of 1935 are fine examples of the *moderne*. The Coca-Cola Bottling Plant of 1936 is designed to resemble a beached ocean liner, a common motif in *moderne* architecture. There are quasi-portholes, decks and nautical railings. Images taken from ocean liners were used again by the same architect, Robert Vincent Derrah, in the design of the Crossroads of the World Shopping Centre in the same year. Derrah had designed the first sound stage for RKO Pictures and had worked with Charlie Chaplin. There was a marked growth in building theatres solely devoted to the exhibition of films, particularly after the introduction of sound, which required great technical support. Key examples include the lavish Warner Western Theatre, now the Wiltern Theatre, and the Warner Beverley Hills Theatre both of 1930, which are traditionally ornate in style and decorated internally with exotic murals and art deco ornament.

However, the most significant impact of the *moderne* style was not in the construction of permanent architecture or buildings able to provoke preservation battles with local art deco societies in the States. While the *moderne* style was felt to represent modernity, science, and the future, and had a currency as a symbol of New Deal America, it also came to prominence at the time of the Depression, when large-scale building was not taking place. It was popular, but also ephemeral, and was commonly used to re-vamp façades of existing commercial buildings – shops, restaurants, cafés and theatres – and also for the mushrooming consumer facilities of supermarkets, bus stations, garages and road-houses of 1930s America. As a consequence, little has survived – it is estimated that 'Probably upward of three-quarters of the Streamline *Moderne* buildings erected in the 1930s are now gone' (Gebhard 1996: 18). Hence, lack of extant examples makes recourse to film or the printed image necessary for an understanding of a style that made modernity acceptable and even exciting to a huge number of people. The *moderne* is preserved for ever on film – the height of its popularity completely in concert with the height of classical Hollywood cinema.

The ways in which classical Hollywood cinema and interior decoration interfaced are also of note when examining the changing nature of glamour. The ostentatious drawing-rooms of New York before the First World War featured in the advice manuals and magazines. By the 1920s little had changed, even after the sets of the 'Our' series made such an impact on the popular imagination. As Joan Crawford commented in relation to the set of her home for *Our Modern Maidens* : 'It's pretty and nice, but it just wouldn't do for our home! . . . Why, look at that archway. Those edges remind me of a buzz-saw, and those windows look just like spider webs. And the floors, with their gold, silver and black paintings, resemble a camouflaged battleship . . . it just wouldn't do as a daily liveable atmosphere' (Crawford 1929 Press Book). A view shared by Cedric Gibbons's film star wife, Doleres Del Rio, who, upon marriage to Gibbons on 6 August 1930 in a Santa Barbara Franciscan mission, insisted on remaining in her Spanish Colonial Revival home in Beverly Hills. However, Gibbons managed to persuade her to move into his *moderne* home in Santa Monica, and the couple were featured at home in *Hollywood* magazine in 1931. The strangeness of the modernistic design of the house is commented upon. It was composed of two flat-roofed rectangles. The interior was *moderne*, with concealed lighting, low couches, shimmering upholstery and semi-abstract sculptures placed in the enormous living-room, which measured twenty-five by forty-five feet. The windows had no curtains in order to show off the *moderne* metal bands and views to the back garden, complete with swimming-pool and tennis courts and the Pacific Ocean beyond. Dolores's dressing-room was lined with mirrors from floor to ceiling; even the covers for the electric switches were mirrored. The publicity shots of the Mexican actress in her dream home reveal a rather ill-at-ease, withdrawn woman. Perched on her *moderne* stool, posing with lipstick brush before a mirror in her dressing-room, she is seen from three angles and looks tense from each. In another shot she sits on a *moderne* seat with reflective metal arms and looks up to Gibbons,

Art deco was used in the design of apartment buildings, corporate headquarters, department stores and film sets to evoke the exclusive ambience of French high style. America had emulated European style since the colonial era and art deco was adopted in the same tradition of emulating European fashion. This came at a time when America was asserting herself as a world power and when the industries upon which her wealth was created – films, electronic goods, cars – were maturing. However, art deco also carried qualities of the *risqué*. This was addressed through the adoption of the *moderne* after 1929 to represent a more futuristic and American image. However, the insecurities created by the Wall Street Crash and the move to isolationism also led Hollywood to focus on a more homely and comfortable image, narrative and set design.

The Battle for Britain

A battle for cultural dominance was played out in Britain during the inter-war years, with the battle lines being distinguished in large part by means of visual style. On one side the trappings and significations of America – Hollywood, modernity, mass consumption, transience, fashion, advertising, leisure and glamour – were ranged against – on the other – European high culture, the International Style, elite taste, authenticity, tradition, lofty moral and political values. The battle lines in Britain were reinforced by social class and gender – women as consumers becoming a major force on the American side, men as producers remaining central to the British (Huyssen 1986). This division has fed into the history of design. The work of the male heroes of the International Style, particularly the architects and their patrons, has been meticulously catalogued and analysed. The experience of the millions – men and women – who attended Odeon cinemas, paddled in the lidos and had fun at Blackpool's Pleasure Beach has been disregarded. The same goes for the design and decoration of the homes in which these millions lived. In an attempt to piece together their experience of glamour I have used family reminiscences, oral histories and contemporary media. Photography, film, fan magazines and professional journals are key materials in tracing the pre-war past; for tracing memories of how things were.

The concept of the atmospheric cinema informed the work of architects and builders in Britain during the late 1920s. However, the atmospheric was also linked with the dreaded Americanization of British culture amongst committed modernists. P. Morton Shand, architectural critic and translator of Walter Gropius's *The New Architecture and the Bauhaus* (1936), complained sarcastically in 1931:

> till quite recently it was a burning question in what style, absence of styles, or jumble of styles, the very latest of 'last words' in super kinemas should be decorated. But the problem was solved almost as soon as it arose. Clearly all that had to be done was to imitate the United States, the home of jazz and all big and fruity things. The Americans, of course, are an ancient people with fine traditions and a wonderful culture; whereas we are only a young . . . nation with nothing very much of our own. Good taste is notoriously a transatlantic monopoly (1931: 4).

Writing in the British decorative arts magazine, *The Studio*, in February 1937, the poet John Betjeman deplored: '. . .the jazz Egyptian of factories by Wallis Gilbert & Partners, and the pseudo-Swedish of the work of Edward Maufe and Grey Wornum, the architects for middle-brows. Textiles show a certain amount of improvement, more often in their texture than their design. But 'jazz' 1925 meaningless juxtaposition of arcs and angles is all too prevalent' (1937: 71). Nikolaus Pevsner, a German *émigré* and supporter of the International Style, conducted a survey of British manufactured goods, which he published in 1937. *An Enquiry into Industrial Art in England* proclaimed with great confidence: '90 per cent of British Industrial art is devoid of any aesthetic merit' (1937: 11). Pevsner singled out the 'Hollywood element' in particular for criticism. He deplored what he labelled jazz modern examples of clock, textile and carpet design. Hollywood in particular was used by the modern design establishment as a metaphor for everything they despised about popular taste. Their perception was that Hollywood cinema and mass-produced, decorative design both somehow 'duped' consumers into consuming passively without rational thought. This was predicated on the notion that their own taste was completely rational, logical and the product of independent judgement. With hindsight, 'form follows function' can seem to be just as much an ideological construct as enjoying the glamour of Hollywood. In fact, conformity to conventions of what constituted a 'proper' cultural activity debarred most design commentators from actually experiencing Hollywood films at first hand, since going to the movies was not part of the social calendar of the intellectual middle and upper classes.

Despite the qualms of the British cultural elite America defined and led glamour during the 1930s in Britain, largely through Hollywood film. This was perceived by many critics as a cultural invasion, or a defection and capitulation. Indeed, Morton Shand criticized the Julian Leathart and W. F. Granger 1929 design for the Richmond Cinema, inspired by the courtyard of a seventeenth-century Spanish nobleman's house, as 'going over to the enemy' (as quoted in Gray 1996: 60). Hollywood glamour was represented throughout the 1930s by the *moderne* and European high culture by modernism. The stylistic vocabulary of the *moderne* was not employed by renowned modern architects, but was created and used by film set designers, interior decorators, commercial artists and local, jobbing architects. It was consumed not by the intellectual elite and respectable upper classes but by the *nouveau riche, outré* photographers and film-makers, *risqué* young aristocrats and a predominately working- and lower-middle-class audiences. It was enjoyed in the provinces and within the feminized commercial and domestic spheres.

It is significant that the histories of the *moderne* and the International Style also reflect these battle lines. The International Style has amassed a significant publishing and exhibition track record. This is reproduced in academic teaching on the subject of the history of architecture and design. Hence, there is a wealth of detailed information and analysis on the work of architects such as Le Corbusier, Mies van der Rohe and Walter Gropius. Every building is carefully catalogued and scrutinized, the travels of the architects are chronicled and their biographies exhaustively reproduced. Their work is internationally recognized and applauded, and has even, retrospectively, become part of popular culture. The Barcelona Pavilion by Mies van der Rohe features in 1998 Citroen television and press adverts along with an Eames chair. However, it is far more difficult to trace the *moderne*, despite the fact that it was one of the more popular styles in Britain during the 1930s. Its shared set of meanings and itinerant architects have not been plotted on the historical map, and the appreciation of its vast audience has hardly been recorded Hence, the discussion of *moderne* architecture that follows centres on the themes of industry and travel, and then considers leisure and pleasure, in an attempt to instate their neglected history.

Ships, Planes and Trains

Following the Wall Street Crash in 1929 Britain, like America, entered a period of economic depression and hardship. Very little building took place between 1930 and 1932. However, a gentle recovery marked the subsequent years leading up to the Second World War, and some 2,700,000 houses were built during the 1930s, 75 per cent by private enterprise. By 1939 one-third of Britain's total housing stock had been built within the preceding twenty years. The concentration of building was in the south of England, particularly in the Greater London area (Oliver, Davis and Bently 1994). Expansion into new industries continued, with the erection of 664 factories in Britain between 1932 and 1937. This growth was in the new industries of car manufacture, artificial fibres, chemicals and electrical goods, less reliant on the export market that had underpinned the more traditional industries of coal-mining, shipbuilding, heavy engineering and iron and steel production. However, this increase in prosperity only affected parts of the country. There was no planned strategy for industrial development, and so the south of England prospered to the detriment of more traditional centres of industry. Of the 664 factories built during the 1930s, over 500 were in Greater London, concentrated around the Great West Road and the North Circular. Key examples include the Hoover, Coty, Pirelli and Brentford Nylon factories. The writer J. B. Priestley remarked at the start of his *English Journey* in 1934:

> After the familiar muddle of West London, the Great West Road looked very odd. Being new, it did not look English. We might have suddenly rolled into California. Or, for that matter, into one of the main avenues of the old exhibition, like the Franco-British Exhibition of my boyhood. It was the line of new factories on each side that suggested the exhibition, for years of the West Riding have fixed for ever my idea of what a proper factory looks like; a grim blackened rectangle with a tall chimney at one corner. . . . At night they look as exciting as Blackpool (1987: 10).

Another major growth area for the building of factories was Croydon, on the southern outskirts of London. Land was divided after the First World War by the government, and the aerodrome built on one half in art deco style in 1928. This is the point from which glamorous Amy Johnson left for her flight to Australia in 1930. The other half of the site was earmarked for factories to accommodate the new, light industries of the inter-war years. The *moderne* cream, flat-roofed buildings lined the new by-pass that carried motor vehicles southwards to the seaside and to Brighton. One example is the steel-framed and concrete factory built by T. Graham Crump in 1933. As in cinemas of the time, there was a key central tower feature, decorated with two long strips of fenestration. The main bulk of the two-storey factory was arranged symmetrically on two sides of the tower, with rounded corners and curved windows running right along the width of the

Figure 27 Oliver P. Bernard, Supermarine Works, Southampton 1937

factory building. The Supermarine Aviation Works at Southampton, designed by Oliver P. Bernard and opened in 1937, used a similar form. The central tower of the administrative block stood over the main entrance, with uninterrupted, vertical windows running up most of its height (Figure 27). The factory building itself had curved corners and horizontal windows that followed the flow of the building. Most of the reinforced concrete building was erected on reclaimed land, and two floors of the rear section extend to the banks of the River Itchen – almost like an ocean liner, complete with miniature mast.

Southampton was the centre for transatlantic travel during the inter-war years. The sheer size of the new type of ocean liner, or floating hotel, meant that the port of Southampton's waters could accommodate their depth. Easy rail travel to London plus proximity to Cherbourg added to the attraction of the port. Southampton was the gateway to the rest of the world, particularly to foreign and exotic locations. Roughly one-third of passengers travelling from the UK to foreign designations travelled via the port of Southampton. In 1937 there were weekly sailings by five separate companies to New York, and Cunard White Star sailed there twice weekly. The way in which the *moderne* style was developed as a dialogue between Europe and America during the 1920s and 1930s relied on this sort of transatlantic travel. The most significant of the ocean liners to leave from Southampton to America was the *Queen Mary*. Built by the British shipping company Cunard, it departed from Southampton on its maiden voyage on 27 May 1936. The ship was a Blue Riband winner: rivalling the French Line's *Normandie*, it symbolized Britain's national pride and resurrection from the Depression. The design of the ship's interior was the responsibility of the New York architect Benjamin Morris, in collaboration with Arthur Joseph Davis of Mewes and Davis, the architects of the Beaux Arts Ritz Hotel and the Royal Automobile Club in London. Cunard's aim was to provide luxurious, transatlantic travel in the most glamorous setting. Competition was fierce on this route, and the more attractive the ships, the more customers could be enticed to travel. As Alan Powers observed: 'the shipping lines of Britain were competing with each other and the rest of the world to produce interiors not only luxurious and chic, but designed by fashionable young architects' (1986: 44). On board one of the most outstanding interiors was the Verandah Grill. Overlooking the sundeck, it was the most fashionable place to be seen during the evening, when it was an *à la carte* restaurant and night-club. There was an extra cover charge for the restaurant, which seated only seventy. The dance floor was parquet, surrounded by black Wilton carpets. The interior decoration was planned by the film and theatre set designer Doris Zinkeisen, and featured a sweeping illuminated balustrade, its colours changing in time with the music. She also painted a mural depicting circus and theatre scenes and ordered the star-studded red velvet curtains. Writing in *Vogue* in 1936, Cecil Beaton observed: 'By far the prettiest room on any ship – becomingly lit, gay in colour and obviously so successful that it would be crowded if twice its present size' (as quoted in Massey 1997: 19). Other interiors of note included the main lounge and cabin-class and tourist-class smoking rooms. The cabin-class featured a polished marble wall covering, decorative rugs and an original painting by Edward Wadsworth entitled *Dressed Overall*. The inclusion of contemporary British art was new for the Cunard Line, and reflected the tastes of Sir Percy Bates, the company's Chairman. Benjamin Morris, assisted by Cunard's Head of Decoration Ernest Leach, selected appropriate artwork for the ship's decoration. Bates then sought the advice of the Director of the National Gallery, Kenneth Clark, and

Grey Wornum, the architect of the RIBA building. Bates rejected the work of Stanley Spencer, McKnight Kauffer and Duncan Grant as too extreme for his appealing luxury floating hotel. This led to criticism from the modernists, particularly critic Clive Bell in *The Listener* (Forsyth 1987).

The design of the ocean liners attracted the same grudging criticism from modernist critics as did the atmospheric cinemas. The *Orion* was a *moderne* Orient Line ship, launched in 1935 to carry passengers to Sydney, Australia. The Modernist critic Geoffrey Grigson chastised the chief designer, Brian O'Rorke, in *The Studio* for compromising on the interior scheme. As with all *moderne* design, it is a mixture of the International Style and art deco. Grigson recounts:

> When I went aboard *Orion* one of the first parts I saw was the library. There they were in neatly designed rectilinear bookcases, Beverley Nicholls, Hugh Walpole, Agatha Christie, J. B. Priestley, Rupert Brooke and, if you please, boldly placed between Honest Rupert and the 'Book of Australasian Verse', the collected poems of Mr. T. S. Eliot. Is this unique in a ship's library? And will it be the one book suspiciously clean when *Orion* first docks in Australia? Anyway, it was a good symbol – Eliot between Brooke and Australasia – of the way in which Mr. O'Rorke and his assistant have outfitted the ship. There is a touch of Corbusier or Gropius between – well, let us be kind – between William Morris and Sir Charles Holden, a pinch of Braque between Paul Nash and Glyn Philpot (1935: 193).

Grigson found the simpler décor of tourist class more to his liking than the sell-out splendour of first-class. O'Rorke also designed the interior of *Orion*'s sister ship, the *Orcades*, for the same route in 1937.

The *Queen Mary's* sister ship, the *Queen Elizabeth*, was launched in 1940 and enjoyed a similar high level of design and finish, produced by Grey Wornum. While films had always been shown on transatlantic journeys since the 1920s by means of a retractable screen in the theatre, the *Queen Elizabeth* had the first purpose-built cinema on board. The cinema was decorated all in white with vibrant red velvet seating specified by Wornum's American wife, Miriam. She was also responsible for the peach velvet curtains in the Verandah Grill and carpets and curtains for the First Class public rooms. Mrs Elizabeth Anne Ede, a driver at Southampton Docks during the 1940s, recalled visiting the *Queen Elizabeth*:

> I was fortunate really to be on the quay and I knew quite a lot of the Berthing Masters there, yes, they took me on board and I was able to wander round. It was a beautiful, beautiful ship, it was the most beautifully built ship that I had seen, then or since . . . all I remember was very, very good quality furniture, fittings and the beautiful workmanship along each side of the corridors where the berths were going off and it was marquetry, all these pictures right the way down the corridors, beautiful workmanship. Everything very good quality, it had a sound to it which was quality. They can say what they like about the ships today, it hasn't got that feeling, to me it is more plastic and different quality materials. In those days it was good wood, beautiful (Massey 1997: 4).

The glamour of cruising was not only promoted through the look of the interiors of the ships, which were featured in advertising and other promotional material, but also through sets of postcards that featured the rooms almost like rooms of stately homes. The image of glamour was also constructed through the photography of Hollywood stars on board the Atlantic ships. When the liners came in to dock, press photographers rushed to catch on film the various celebrities as they disembarked. Stars were frequently photographed boarding the train at Terminus Station for London. Margaret Florence Green, who worked on the Docks Telephone Exchange during the 1950s, recalls:

> It was an exciting time: it was really, really glamorous, because I think from just after the war going through this era was such a change that it really was; and if you had somebody that worked on the *Queen Mary*, the film stars coming through or speaking to them on the docks, you really felt as though you were part of a glamorous era (Massey 1997: 7).

Southampton was also the home of the Schneider Trophy. At nearby Calshot, Great Britain's High Speed Flight team retained the trophy in September 1931, with the new world record of 386.1 m.p.h. The flying boats that carried passengers to South America also left from Southampton, and the posters for travel by this novel and glamorous method used the familiar, smooth and streamlined lines of the *moderne*. Air travel was in its infancy at this point, more a source of glamour and aspiration than actual experience for most. The depiction of aircraft in Hollywood film reinforced this image. New airports were built during the inter-war years, which also borrowed from this imagery. As airports, like cinemas, were a new building type, architects used the contemporary vocabulary of what was stylish and appealing. The airport at

Croydon opened in 1928, the former makeshift sheds replaced by smart, art deco buildings. At Gatwick the famous Beehive Building was built in 1936. Planned by Hoar, Marlow and Lovett on a six-sided outline, it provided a space for waiting passengers and mobile passageways that led straight to the waiting aeroplanes. Passageways like this had been in use in California since the end of the 1920s, but this was their first use in Britain. At Ramsgate, D. Pleydell-Bouverie designed the municipal airport in 1937. Intended to be as recognizable from the air as by land, the shape was that of an aeroplane, with two wings tapering away on either side of a central observation tower. The *moderne* influence can be detected in the decision to include a horizontal strip of glass right along the airfield side of the building and wrap around the curved corners at each tip. There was also a streamlined banister tracing the edges of either side of the building. At Southampton a new airport building was erected in 1932. Nearby, the Cuncliffe-Owen Aircraft Factory was opened in 1939. The building was constructed from steel-frame reinforced concrete, with a brick fascia. As the local newspaper noted on the opening of the factory:

> Designed on modernistic lines, the administrative block faces north. Brown brick facings relieved with bands of artificial stone rendering in cream, give the facade an attractive finish. A striking feature is the canopy of reinforced concrete, 55ft in length and projecting eight feet over the main doorway in the middle of the block, which is 212 ft long. The canopy has been built on the cantilever principle. A revolving door gives access to the handsome foyer, paved in green terrazzo, as also are the ground floor corridors (25 January 1939: 3).

Great play was made of the use of specially diffused lighting for the buildings. It was noted that the kitchen that served the works canteens was: 'planned on the most modern lines, and full equipment includes such things as automatic washing-up machines and potato peelers' (25 January 1939: 3). A touch of excitement was added for the official opening when the American test pilot for the company, Clyde Pangborn, was scheduled to fly the prototype flying wing aircraft to the new factory. Alas, bad weather made the flight impossible.

While the newest form of transport was certainly the aeroplane, this remained an elite method. Much more accessible was travel by train. Great play was made of the speed of train travel in the 1930s, with the *Mallard* breaking all records for steam locomotives on 7 July 1938 by reaching a speed of 126 m.p.h. Travel from the north to the south of the country was eased by trains like the *Silver Jubilee,* introduced in 1935, which sped between Newcastle and London in a record four hours. A 1935 poster for the journey, designed by Frank Newbould, emphasized that this was 'Britain's First Streamline Train'. Its advertised average speed was 67.08 m.p.h., and record speeds of 112.5 m.p.h. were reached during the journey (Figure 28). Car ownership also increased during the 1930s, although it never reached American levels. For most working-class British families in the 1930s, cars were increasingly seen, but seldom owned. My mother's uncle was the first in her family to own a car, and that was after the Second World War. My paternal grandfather never owned a car, nor did my father-in-law, walking, the bus, bicycles, trams, trains or motor-cycles being the normal modes of transport during the 1930s. My father recalled: 'Never owned a car, correct. Did own motor cycles. My mother and father used to zoom off when I was young – 5 or 6, before the war. He dressed in black leather coat and helmet and my mother in white' (Interview with author 1998). In architectural terms car ownership, particularly in the south of England, necessitated new forms of building in the shape of road-houses, car showrooms, petrol stations and garages.

A series of car service stations was designed by Cameron Kirby and built throughout London. The cinematic influence can be observed here, thus: 'The aim of the architect has been to obtain a design which, although varying for each individual site, retains two features observable in them all. These features are the tower, and the wide-span shop-front' (*The Architects' Journal*, 4 October 1934: 493). The huge expanse of the shop-front was equipped with a sliding-folding door to allow cars to be taken in and out. The building was steel-framed and faced in artificial Portland stone. A service station at Catford by the same architect built in 1935 featured the same folding-sliding doors and a tower that was decorated with neon lighting, indicating that this was 'Morris House'. Another new building type to result from the more widespread use of cars was the road-house – a pub or restaurant situated at the roadside. Many were built during the 1930s in the new suburban areas, usually in mock-Tudor style to represent the romantic image of 'Ye Olde England' and the friendly tavern. However, some were constructed in *moderne* style. The Showboat at Maidenhead was the most extensive. Constructed entirely from reinforced concrete, it opened in 1933. Designed by D. C. Wadhwa and E. Norman Bailey, it boasted a car park at the front, a large swimming-pool, a restaurant, a ballroom, tea and sun-bathing terraces, a club-room and a bar. A smaller example is Chez Laurie at Herne Bay, built in 1937, which featured a decorative mural

Figure 28 LNER Poster 'Silver Jubilee' 1935, Frank Newbould

illustrating different phases of travel. The building, by W. M. Bishop, had a central three-storey tower with a mast that sported the large insignia of Chez Laurie. The single-storey lounge and dining-room featured curved corners with windows. Oliver Hill's Prospect Inn at Minster in Thanet, Kent featured a planned car park and space for charabancs far bigger than the actual inn itself. It was built from a brick and steel frame with a flat, reinforced concrete roof. On the roof was a white reinforced concrete pylon, which was floodlit at night and topped by a neon star.

Leisure in Style

While the spread of the suburbs and the expansion of car ownership are indicative of recovery and a measure of prosperity in the South, in North-East England the picture of working-class life was different. The coalfields of the North-East of England, which my family relied on for jobs, were hard hit by shrinkage in the export market and decline in heavy industry. During the General Strike of 1926 my grandmother remembered picking wild blackberries with her miner brothers to help stave off hunger pangs. Just before the Jarrow Crusade in 1936 both my grandmothers left home to work in the more affluent areas of England – Manchester and Hampshire. They were sent 'to place', as it was known at the time – which was how my maternal grandmother continued to refer to working away from home as a housemaid throughout her life. They cared little for the debates around the modern movement that were developing at that time and were broadcast on the new BBC Radio service or discussed in the pages of professional journals like *Architectural Review* or *The Studio*. What provided excitement and enjoyment to young women like these in the 1930s was Hollywood glamour and new forms of leisure pursuits that were imported from America. Both could dance the Charleston and both were photographed wearing Hollywood-inspired clothes, hair and make-up. The sleek *moderne* as seen on the cinema screens carried with it the hope of a brighter future, a future underpinned by the values of modernity. Mass production seemed to promise consumer goods for all, and mass leisure facilities new types of fun for everyone, one of the most important being cinema.

The Odeon chain was the most prolific chain of cinemas to emerge during the 1930s, its owner, Oscar Deutsch, opening 142 cinemas nation-wide between 1930 and the outbreak of the Second World War. Many were built in the new suburban areas to cater for the lower-middle-class patron. Housing developments at Tolworth in Surrey and Colindale, North London were enhanced by the addition of a new Odeon. The cinemas had a distinctive house style, which was *moderne*. The exteriors were often clad in cream tile to emphasize the smooth, horizontal lines of the facade. This horizontal emphasis was frequently complemented by a striking vertical feature. This was usually illuminated at night, and carried the Odeon name in its distinctive, squared-off lettering. The central tower feature was first used in the design of Dreamland at Margate, Kent in 1935, and was featured heavily in the architectural press. Designed by Leahart and Granger, Dreamland replaced the original music hall, which had doubled up as a cinema but had been destroyed by fire in 1931. The soaring, aerodynamic fin tower was built in brick, but carried the Dreamland title vertically. Gray suggests that this practice had been developed in America and was then adopted by the architects at Margate, which seems likely (1996: 93). The fin is sandwiched between two stepped-back, vertical features, a motif again adopted by the Odeon chain from 1935 onwards with the design of the Kingstanding, Birmingham Odeon of 1935, where the architect used a row of three vertical fins. The flagship for the Odeon chain was built in Leicester Square, London and opened in 1937. Faced in dramatic, polished granite, it had a tower set asymmetrically to the left that carried the familiar Odeon lettering. Designed to be seen at night, the geometric outline of the building was picked out in neon light with illuminated lettering advertising the film on show. Inside, the auditorium featured mock leopard-skin seats and a ribbed, arched ceiling with phased lighting. *The Times* reviewer attended the opening of the cinema and felt rather threatened by the new auditorium, which:

> gives the impression of being made from a single piece of material. Its walls are uniformly gilded, for the most part, without ornament, but with ribs which make a continuous curve up the walls, across the ceiling, and down again. These curves have, no doubt, some structural function, but it is not immediately apparent and one might suspect instead some mysterious acoustic properties. In fact the whole construction gives one the sensation of being enclosed inside a machine, the horn of a gramophone, or the entrails of a loud-speaker ominously shaped so that the sound will reverberate around the victim (3 November 1937: 17).

The drive to improve the image of going to the pictures was certainly aided by the opening of the Leicester Square Odeon, showing *The Prisoner of Zenda* and with the Duke and Duchess of Gloucester, Viscount and Viscountess Hailsham, the Duke and Duchess of Marlborough and more than thirty other members of the British aristocracy plus various MPs in attendance.

Beside the Sea

Apart from the new suburban areas and prestigious city-centre developments, many cinemas were built as part of leisure complexes at the seaside. For the first time all workers benefited from a break from work with pay, thanks to the Holidays with Pay Act of 1938. Before that,

Figure 29 My Mother at the Seaside (centre) with my Grandmother (to her left), 1939

day trips to the seaside by train or charabanc were popular. A coach would be hired for a whole village, works or organization. These day trips were still popular in the 1960s. My own family would go by coach on a day trip organized by the British Legion from Consett in County Durham to Whitley Bay for the day (Figure 29). Purpose-built complexes were erected around the coast of Britain to cater for the expanding trade. Prior to this entertainment revolved around the pier, with 'What the Butler Saw' machines and Punch and Judy shows and films shown in makeshift tents. The Dreamland cinema at Margate was part of a larger entertainment complex on the seafront. At Lee-on-Solent, the New Pier Buildings were erected in 1935–6 next to the old pier and railway station. The complex comprised a pavilion, a restaurant, a bar, a winter garden, an amusement hall and a cinema. The design of the buildings resembled an ocean liner, the ultimate icon of pleasure. Its central tower reached one hundred feet into the sky, complete with observation platform accessible by lift. The architects, Yates, Cook and Darbyshire, also designed the Odeon cinemas at Worcester Park, Tolworth and Wallington.

Day trips to Blackpool were popular amongst the northern mill workers and mining families from the late nineteenth century onwards. My paternal grandmother took a coach trip to see Blackpool illuminations every year in November. Blackpool developed as a holiday and leisure destination after the railway arrived there in 1863, the same year in which the first pier was erected. The Winter Gardens, the Opera House and the famous Tower were all added in the late nineteenth century. The Pleasure Beach was completely American-inspired. It was founded at the turn of the century by W. G. Bean, in partnership with John W. Outhwaite. Bean had worked as an engineer in a New York amusement park in the late nineteenth century, and aimed: 'to found an American style amusement park, the fundamental principle of which is to make adults feel like children again, and to inspire gaiety of a primary innocent character' (quoted in Stansfield 1986: 15). The Big Dipper was introduced in 1922; the Grand National – Europe's only roller coaster with two tracks – opened in 1935, and was designed by the architect Joseph Emberton. Bean's son-in-law, Leonard Thompson, decided to modernize the Park and approached Emberton to produce designs, which included one for rebuilding the Casino at the entrance to the park, which was in a dated Indian style. Emberton and Thompson travelled to America to glean the latest ideas about amusement park planning. At that time America was held to be the best at the design of such activities, the native home of amusement and entertainment in general, beyond just Hollywood. The main feature of the revamp was the remodelled Casino, which actually functioned as a restaurant because of restrictions on gaming. Completed in 1938, it was built from reinforced concrete. The sweeping curves of the circular main building contrasted with the tower, which consisted of a glass cylinder encasing a spiral staircase. It featured a further corkscrew above the entrance, which carried the title of 'Casino' vertically. The sweeping curves of the window bands afforded a panoramic view of the park and the seafront promenade; and this plus the American inspiration made it a prime example of the *moderne* style.

American amusements also inspired the British showman Billy Butlin to import dodgem cars into Britain from America in 1928, well before he established his popular holiday camps. He then became the European distributor for these streamlined little cars, which spun across the polished metal floor and bumped madly into each other. Butlin owned amusement parks at Hayling Island, Bognor, Felixstowe, Portsmouth, Bexhill and the Isle of Man. Butlin's first holiday camp, based on his Canadian experiences, opened at Skegness in 1936. Built in *moderne* style, it offered accommodation in chalets and entertainment in the ballroom, ice-rink and games room. The American Cocktail Bar was decked out with tubular steel furniture, including cantilevered chairs, mirrors and sophisticated lighting. Touches of glamour were added by the appearance of British film stars, including the ever-popular Gracie Fields at the theatre. Another camp was opened at Clacton in 1938, with exactly the same *moderne* buildings and furniture to provide holidays for 5,400 happy campers. Tented camps had existed before Butlin opened Skegness, but: 'The difference was that Butlin added to the formula the panache of his long experience as a showman and immense success as an operator of amusement parks, the glamour of the same kind of luxury that was found in the super cinemas of the 1930s, and the thrill of seeing entertainers and sporting celebrities whose names were household words' (Ward: 1986: 57–8). Similar holiday camps were established by Harry Warner on Hayling Island in 1930, followed by three others before the outbreak of war.

For the more upmarket holiday-maker, hotels were built at seaside resorts in the *moderne* style. At Morecambe, just north of Blackpool, an important *moderne* hotel was built for the London Midland and Scottish Railway Company, opposite the Victorian station and replacing a demolished Victorian hotel. Designed by the leading *moderne* architect, Oliver Hill, the Midland Hotel opened in June 1933 (Figure 30). The motive for using Hill to design the hotel was to attract a more sophisticated, younger set to Morecambe, which attracted the same type of day-trippers as Blackpool. The design of the hotel was thus in keeping with the new, young spirit of modernity that inspired the building of new luxurious cinemas and relaxed country retreats. The sweeping frontage of the three-storey hotel faced the station, while the convex rear, complete with balconies and recreation areas, overlooked the sea. The building was white rendered cement, with the sweeping lines of the main façade emphasized by four horizontal bands, painted in brilliant green. The nautical analogy was prevalent, as *Architectural Review* noted: 'It rises from the sea like a great white ship, gracefully curved, like a great Venus Anadyomene in white cement' (September 1933). The main entrance features a cinematic tower, decorated with three long vertical metal framed windows topped by two decorative seahorses carved by Eric Gill.

The entrance opened into the main foyer, with a spiral staircase with a metal handrail reminiscent of that seen in *Grand Hotel*, leading to forty bedrooms, and culminating in a relief, also by Gill, depicting the son of Neptune. The hotel was stylishly furnished throughout, as

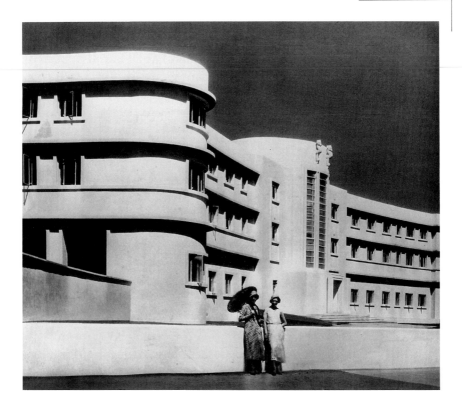

Figure 30 Oliver Hill, Midland Hotel, Morecambe, 1931–2

specified by Hill, who had been working largely as an interior decorator during the1920s. There were Marion Dorn rugs and textiles by Allan, Walton, Duncan Grant and Frank Dobson. The two hand-knotted, circular rugs Dorn designed for the foyer measured fifteen feet six inches or five metres in diameter, and their strong, interlocking lines echoed the waves of the sea. The rugs decorated a floor made of polished cement terrazzo inlaid with silver glass mosaic – catching the light and glinting like the sea. Hill designed the furniture for the hotel in weathered sycamore and tubular steel. He went on to remodel the interiors of the Euston Hotel in London and to design an American Bar for St Pancras, this form of sleek *moderne* being regarded as embodying the attractive features that upmarket young clients sought.

The Midland Hotel still operates as a hotel, but is sadly dilapidated. The *moderne* interiors have all but disappeared along with the furniture and furnishings, replaced by broken-down velour three-piece suites.

The exterior is showing signs of wear, with ugly rust stains running down the previously pristine exterior. However, the market for glamorous breaks on the northern coast of England has all but disappeared. As the American journalist Bill Bryson observed during his travels around Britain:

> Today the hotel is gently crumbling around the edges and streaked here and there with rust stains. Most of the original interior fittings were lost during periodic and careless refurbishments over the years, and several large Eric Gill statues that once graced the entranceway and public rooms simply disappeared, but it still has an imperishable 1930s charm. . . . As I was departing, my eye was caught by a large white plaster statue by Gill of a mermaid in the empty dining room. I went and had a look at it and found that the tail of the statue, which I presume is worth a small fortune, was held on with a mass of sticky tape. It seemed a not inappropriate symbol for the town (1995: 273–4).

In a better state of repair is a prime *moderne* hotel to be found in Bournemouth. Situated on the south coast of England, the former health retreat developed rapidly as a seaside resort during the inter-war years. As one contemporary commentator observed: 'We see her as a modern child, of modern times, without the legacies of a world of yester-year. She was created as a Resort. She has never known an existence other than as a holiday resort' (Birtwistle 1934: 55). The population of Bournemouth was 695 in 1851, rising to 16,859 in 1881 and over 120,000 in 1934 – summer visitors would double this figure. Bournemouth flourished as a resort just at the time when Hollywood glamour defined the *moderne*, and so it contains far more *moderne* buildings than the more traditional resorts of Brighton or Worthing.

This was a source of regret for some locals. Writing in the *Bournemouth Western Post and Graphic* in 1935, a local journalist described the Palace Court Hotel:

> The huge modern building on the left, now nearing completion, dwarfs the pine trees and occupies the site of one or more of the picturesque detached villas which formerly extended along the Westover Road. These villas were some of the first to be built in the town, and may well have been in Thomas Hardy's mind when he wrote his famous description of "Sandbourne" in "Tess of the D'Urbervilles." . . . But the old villas have all gone, and perhaps no part of Bournemouth has changed so rapidly, and so completely as the portion we illustrate (25 May 1935) (Figure 31).

Figure 31 A. J. Seal & Partners, Palace Court Hotel, Bournemouth

Designed by the local architectural practice A. J. Seal and Partners, the Palace Court Hotel displays the key features of the *moderne* style. It is a 110-foot steel-framed building (one of the highest in Bournemouth at the time), entirely faced in brick but rendered in white plaster with a flat roof. The concrete balconies make up the distinctive parallel sweeping lines on seven levels of the façade. Seen from the street, the undulations of the balconies, the way in which they sweep forward and then back, is animated – almost like waves of the sea. This is further emphasized by the horizontal, parallel lines cast into the balconies at either side of the second floor. The fenestration consists of metal window frames, curved at the corners to echo the form of the balconies. The name of the hotel is clearly signalled with simple but stylish, sans serif black lettering on the first-floor sun terrace, which runs the entire width of the building. The entrance is given emphasis at ground level with a canopy which leads into a glamorous foyer area, complete with shops.

The symbols of modernity were the key to this *moderne* design – the hotel was floodlit in colour by night and boasted 1,500 electric lights in total. Every room or flat had a telephone and a radio – a huge radio set dominated the hotel lounge – all running from the same central aerial. *The Architect and Building News* reported : 'An especial feature is the wireless installation in the public rooms, controlled from the manager's office so that it can be used not only for music, but for general announcements and in place of the clumsy "call-boy" system' (10 January 1936: 67). The heating of the building was completely up to date, with central heating and radiators with supplementary, voguish electric fires. It was noted in *The Architects' Journal* that: 'Points have been placed on landing, services, and all flats for portable vacuum cleaning apparatus, this system being considered the most suitable for this particular building' (9 January 1936: 49). It is worth bearing in mind that vacuum cleaners had only recently been widely adopted for commercial and domestic use from America as a labour-saving device.

The characteristics of the interior are also typical of the *moderne* style. The highly polished wooden flooring in the public areas was adorned with strongly patterned rugs or fitted carpet. Rubber was used to cover the floors of the bathrooms and kitchenettes in the service flats on the fifth to ninth floors. New materials were used to decorate the walls, including sprayed on, textured cement, and stainless metal for skirting and grilles contrasted with vast areas of peach-tinted mirror. The atmosphere of high luxury was enhanced by concealed lighting. Fittings and furniture in the public areas, for example the first-floor club with lounge, recreation room and cocktail bar – another key feature of the *moderne* interior – were again sweeping in form, emphasizing the curvilinear as opposed to the geometric (Figure 32). The columns were decorated in gold, complemented by dramatic scarlet and fawn. The radiator grilles were constructed from chromium tube, as were the bar stools. Furniture was made from polished metal or exotic wood and covered with sumptuous, brightly coloured textiles. In the bedrooms, the twin beds were always adorned by satin bedspreads (Figure 33). Other furniture included bedside cabinets doubling as telephone stands, and the *de rigueur* dressing-table. Typical *moderne* bedrooms always had a balcony, as did those at the Palace Court Hotel, to allow the occupant(s) to benefit fully from the open air. On the seventh floor, the four penthouse flats had huge sundecks that emulated the experience of walking on the deck of an ocean liner, with the same handrails and uninterrupted view of the sea. The bathrooms were always a prime feature of the *moderne* interior, with mirrors, full-tiling in pink or green, concealed lighting and a shiny, coloured porcelain suite shaped in sensuous, curved forms.

Figure 32 Palace Court Hotel Cocktail Bar

Like many of the buildings included in this book, information about the architect or the history of the commissioning and building of the Palace Court Hotel was difficult to locate, although the architect was praised just after the opening of the hotel by the trade journal, *The Architect and Building News* (1936) as 'an architect who may truly be said to have altered the face of Bournemouth. Mr. Seal's work, which we have illustrated from time to time during the last few years, has always been characterised by a freshness and originality both in design and planning and, particularly, in all those various details which add lustre and interest to a building' (1936: 65). This was not the type of avant-garde, modernist piece of 'high architecture' that would grace the pages of professional magazines like the *Architectural Review* or feature in architectural exhibitions at the RIBA or in conventional histories of modern architecture or design. The building, or the work of the architect, has not received any further coverage since its opening, apart from in the local newspaper.

The growth of Bournemouth and its locality during the 1930s is clear from the other buildings that line the municipal park and seafront.

Figure 33 Palace Court Hotel, Bedroom

The most outstanding *moderne* buildings are designed by Seal, including the *Daily Echo* Offices, home of the local newspaper and built in 1933–4. The entrance is crowned by a square tower, punctuated by three vertical bands of glass. On either side the offices are stepped down, with flat roofs, and the building curves around the corner, with stripped windows that match the curve. The same curved corners can be found on the Theatre Chambers, also by Seal and built 1932–3, and the Bournemouth Gas and Water Company offices in nearby Boscombe of 1935–6. The Pearl Assurance Building by McGrath and Goodesmith stands on a corner site and looks much as did when it was built in 1937. It is a six-storey building, faced in cream tile with a nautical rail adorning the top of the fifth level. The building has the familiar curved corner with curved windows to add emphasis. The main entrance is asymmetrical, with the cream stone set off by a bronze circular ventilating grille and delicate bronze lettering above the door. Other remnants of Bournemouth's pre-war growth remain, some virtually derelict and carrying 'To Let' signs, some well preserved, like the Beales department store.

The growth in popularity of the seaside for day trips or longer holidays and the promotion of the healthy outdoors as a whole also led to the building of outdoor swimming and children's paddling pools throughout Britain during the 1930s. Built in suburban and seaside locations, the outdoor pools enabled the working and lower middle classes to engage in the healthy pursuit of outdoor swimming. More wealthy swimmers were members of private health clubs or had their own pools. Outdoor pools were built in the rapidly expanding suburb of Croydon in Surrey. The Purley Way swimming pool was opened in 1935 and was 200 feet long and 70 feet wide. It could accommodate 1,200 people, and contemporary photographs show a predominantly young crowd – roughly the same age group who regularly attended the cinema – swimming, watching or lying on the surrounding grass in one-piece bathing costumes (Figure 34). The pools were usually constructed from concrete or artificial stone with *moderne* decorative touches, including standing lights and fountains. Pools were often built as part of a lido complex. Named after the island and bathing beach near Venice, they included other forms of entertainment. The London County Council pioneered the building of pools in the early 1930s, with examples built in both the Victoria and Brockwell Parks, followed by seven more. Soon similar developments sprung up as municipal projects in various parks of England, other popular pools being built at Roehampton in 1934, Petersfield, Sussex in 1935 and places like Ilkley, Norwich, Finchley, Peterborough, Saltdean, Hilsea near Portsmouth and Aylesbury. The Penzance Jubilee Pool was officially opened in 1935, and included a huge pool, filled naturally by seawater, but also high diving boards, areas for sunbathing and facilities for concerts. It was triangular in shape, and the addition of metal railings echoed the prow of an ocean liner. The pool was also floodlit to enable late-night swimming. A great asset to the town, it was perceived at the time as replacing the old lime kiln and slum housing with a facility which would be: 'a source of health, strength and pleasure to all who made full use of it' (*Cornishman and Cornish Telegraph* 1935: 4). The style of the lido was *moderne*, with sweeping curves and emphasis on horizontal features. As the local paper reported: 'The monotony of straight walls and right angles – the domain of the compass and ruler – has been entirely and utterly avoided. Instead, there are graceful curves and pleasing lines – an adaptation of cubism to the terraces and diving platforms which enhances the effect and makes the whole so pleasing to the eye.' Designed by the Borough Engineer, Capt. Frank Latham, it has recently been saved and restored to its original glory thanks to the

Figure 34 Purley Way Swimming Pool, 1936

efforts of retired architect John Clarke and funding from English Heritage, The European Regional Development Fund and Penzance Town Council. However, many of the lidos have since been demolished, to be replaced by indoor swimming pools or leisure centres.

The sporting, outdoor life gained popularity in the 1930s, particularly among the under-30s. The restrictive lifestyles of Edwardian Britain, where a trip to the seaside would involve keeping hat, gloves and long-sleeved, full-length dresses on, shaded by a parasol, to avoid getting an unfashionable sun tan, were outdated. Bathing in the sea would only take place from a bathing carriage pulled into the sea, and only when one was clothed in a swimming costume from neck to ankle. The major transformation that took place in the 1930s was that leisure, including visiting the seaside or bathing outdoors, was made available for all. There were far fewer restrictions on clothing, and a suntan was positively fashionable, possibly as a result of the discovery of vitamin D. The fashion was also reinforced by Hollywood films, which featured bathing scenes and wholesome sports as part of their more respectable image during the 1930s. Apart from swimming, golf proved another popular outdoor activity reinforced by Hollywood. In 1938 the mass-circulation women's magazine, *Home Chat*, revealed: 'Fred (MacMurray) is tremendously popular with filmland's sporting colony. Tennis and swimming are his chief sports – but Bing Crosby has just lured him to a golf course!' Hollywood stars emulated the wealthy and the aristocracy in playing the game of golf, particularly the example of the Duke of Windsor. The wealthy played 18-hole courses at Wentworth in Surrey or coastal settings like Hayling Island or Royal Birkdale in Lancashire, with new clubhouses built in the 1930s to accommodate the growing membership and the need for better facilities. Often designed by local architects, the clubhouse used the stylistic vocabulary of the *moderne* to denote leisure and glamour. At Birkdale the original, largely one-storey clubhouse was replaced in 1935 by a *moderne* luxury building. Designed by the local architect, George Tonge, it is flat-roofed, clad in white rendering with touches of ocean liner, and situated in the dunes overlooking the eighteenth hole and the sea beyond by means of a magnificent, curved bay window. Local commentators noted: 'As Birkdale is a seaside course, the architect, Mr. George Tonge, of Southport, has designed a building which fits on the sandhills like a cruiser on the waves. Its stories [*sic*] resemble the decks of a ship. Standing on the Promenade Deck overlooking the Irish sea, it needs little imagination to feel that one is on a cruise' (The Royal Birkdale Club, 1998: 14). Tonge also designed a luxury house on the edge of the course in the same *moderne* style. Similar developments took place on the Wentworth site in Surrey, with luxury mansions built around the edge of the course in *moderne* style. More downmarket were the pitch-and-put greens and American-inspired crazy golf areas at seaside resorts, often overlooked, as they are at Whitley Bay, by flat-roofed, *moderne* semi-detached houses.

At Home with Modernity

The lure of the outdoor life and the theme of the ocean liner inspired the design of private houses and apartment block buildings during the 1930s in Britain, particularly in coastal and suburban areas. Like the hotels discussed already, they frequently featured balconies for sunbath-ing, sun terraces or even sleeping porches. Geographically, *moderne* houses were most frequently constructed in the more prosperous south of England, with very few examples in the north of the country. They were always financed privately, and ranged from the modest semi-detached, two-storey dwelling in the suburbs to the glamorous country retreats of film-makers and architects further afield. Usually the *moderne* style was not adopted wholesale for suburban development, but was often the minority style, featured cheek-by-jowl with houses in the popular Tudor revival or Georgian Revival styles.

There is a considerable blurring of distinction between the modern and the *moderne* when it comes to house design. Whereas in Britain the strictures of the pure International Style found little popularity for public buildings or hotels, for private dwellings, particularly weekend retreats, it did have some resonance among the liberal middle classes. For the purposes of this account, *moderne* houses are defined as those featuring curved corner windows, flat roofs and decorative elements on the exterior, particularly the use of bright colours. Such windows were so ubiquitous because of their availability by means of mass fabrication and supply by distributors such as the Crittall Metal Window Company or Williams and Williams. Jeremy Gould has produced an invaluable *Gazetteer of Modern Houses in the United Kingdom and the Republic of Ireland* (1996) that includes all private houses built in Britain between the wars with flat roofs: hence his survey includes modern and *moderne*. Gould's main sources are contemporary journals and books, and so the examples included tend to be of the more upmarket and aesthetically significant variety, which would necessarily be featured in the press. Work by purist modernists such as Connell, Ward & Lucas or Walter Gropius is included along with the lesser-known *moderne* work of A. J. Seal in Bournemouth. Gould classifies all examples as Modern, and confesses: 'a flat roof is in general here taken as the criterion for inclusion in the gazetteer. Beyond that, no stylistic bar has been applied, so that good, bad and indifferent are all listed together' (1996: 112). Many of the houses listed by Gould were built for private, wealthy patrons. Louise Campbell has demonstrated that such patrons sought to commission modern homes as a form of revolt against their backgrounds and upbringing (1996). Modernism in general was associated with left-wing politics and radical behaviour before and just after the Second World War in the mass media. Figures such as the wealthy Roland Penrose rebelled against their upper-class backgrounds by using their extensive resources to support little-known modern artists such as Picasso and Max Ernst, staging the International Surrealist Exhibition in London in 1937 and flirting with communism (Massey 1995). A debate in the letters page of the *Architects' Journal* acts as an indication of prevailing attitudes. The debate was over the refusal of planning consent for Connell and Ward's elevations for two houses by Ruislip-Northwood Urban District Council. Daniel Roth defended the decision, revealing something of his own prepossessions in the process: 'Although we may consider them somewhat conservative (a failing which is notoriously on the right side) . . .'. He also dismissed the prevalent notion that all modern architects were under thirty years old and that the panel was offended by the 'foreign' origin of the modern style of the designs (*Architects' Journal*, 5 July 1934: 12). It is therefore easy to understand why patrons such as Jack and Frances Donaldson, who commissioned Gropius to design Wood House at Shipbourne for them in 1937, considered themselves radical in their support of modern architecture. Frank Donaldson worked as secretary at the Pioneer Health Centre at Peckham, and the decision to engage Gropius came from the couple's shared philanthropic values, as Frances Donaldson recalled: 'We decided in an almost crusading spirit that the only intelligent thing was to build in the architectural style of our own day. This crusading spirit almost completely prevented me from asking myself whether I actually liked it' (quoted in Campbell 1996: 46). Apart from rebelling against the prevailing norms of middle-class society, clients for modern architecture such as this were also part of a vital network of other, like-minded intellectuals and architects. It certainly was radical to live in a modern house during this period, as the popular reception of the modern movement in Britain, lampooned in newspaper cartoons and often falling foul of strict planning laws, was openly hostile.

Moderne houses were less severe and depended less for their effect on the stark emptiness of interior spaces; perhaps this is why they seem to have been considered more fun and were certainly more popular than the stricter angles and straight lines of the modern. Clients were less purist and less radical, and wanted something fashionable and fun to live in when they commissioned a *moderne* house, frequently near the sea for weekend and holiday use. For example, there were tremendous developments in seaside dwellings during the 1930s on the Essex coast. Beginning in 1927–8 with the developments at Silver End by Crittall, the manufacturer of metal windows, developments followed at Holland on Sea, Frinton-on-Sea, Hadleigh and Westcliff-on-Sea. At Holland-on-Sea a three-bedroomed house was built facing the sea for a London businessman to use at weekends. Designed by Ronald Franks, it comprised three solids – the garage, a one-storey lounge and then upper-storey bedrooms. The one-storey lounge, with its curved metal corner window, afforded a panoramic view of the sea and the terrace just outside. Placed perilously near the cliffs, the all-white house looked like a boat that had been washed up by the tide. 'White Walls' at Torquay (1931) had a similar appearance, with a flat roof covered with Ruberoid and concrete paving to enable sunbathing. There was even a second-floor 'roof bedroom' with south-facing windows covering its

Figure 35 A. J. Seal & Partners, Conning Tower, Poole Harbour

entire width, shaded by a curved, tiled canopy. Overlooking Torbay it was one of 24 *moderne* houses to be built in Torquay during the 1930s.

Bournemouth and nearby Poole, as part of their inter-war expansion, also feature many examples of *moderne* private houses (Figure 35). The sea view was certainly a defining feature of these expensive, specially commissioned homes. The Harbour Heights estate by A. J. Seal and Partners, just west of Bournemouth overlooking Poole Harbour, is one of the most striking developments. It included the Harbour Heights Hotel, two residential blocks, The Haven and Conning Tower, plus Haven Close, which consisted of two rows of single-storey, flat-roofed terraced houses. Conning Tower was a huge residence spreading on to four floors, featured only in *Architect and Building News* at the time of construction on 21 August 1936. The shell was redeveloped during 1998 into nine luxury apartments. Pevsner commented on the original development: 'The buildings are admirably sited, with prominent glazed staircase curves derived from Mendelsohn; but the detailing everywhere degenerates into what Betjeman calls the Tel-Aviv style' (1972: 332).

Constructed of steel frame with white, rendered brick walls, Conning Tower was built originally for Sam Goodman. The house boasted a cinema measuring 32 by 14 feet, a cocktail bar and a billiards room on the lower-ground floor. On the ground floor was the magnificent living space, with a projecting sun lounge with magnificent views of the harbour and glazed doors opening on to the sun terrace. The first floor consisted of six bedrooms, a night nursery and four bathrooms. The en-suite bathroom for the main bedroom featured a black porcelain enamelled bath, wash basin, toilet and bidet. Two other bathrooms featured a primrose yellow and a pink suite, while the maid's bathroom was a more utilitarian white. The three floors were connected by means of a spiral staircase encased in a ribbed glass tower, which also led on to a flat roof, partially covered and designed to be used for sunbathing.

Other *moderne* seaside retreats of note near Poole Harbour included a house known as Showboat, designed by A. J. Seal and Partners for Seal himself. Pevsner was less impressed with this building than he had been with the Harbour Heights development: 'Showboat opposite is also stepped back, but only on its façade, and in a facetious symmetry appropriate to its name. Amongst all this jazz it is surprising to find a sensitive Voyseysish villa dated 1911 . . .' (1972: 332). Seal admired the popular music allusions of his seaside weekend retreat. According to *The Architect and Building News*, when he first saw the building in 1931 without its scaffolding he commented: 'It looks like a musical comedy setting' (12 February 1932: 228). Seal, unlike the strict modernist Pevsner, appeared to revel in the light-hearted nature of the retreat, and had the name Showboat placed above the main entrance. The light-hearted nature of the buildings was further enhanced by the white rendered wall accentuated by the bright green window frames and yellow sunblinds. There was a purpose-built sun terrace on the roof and a balcony leading from the main bedroom. Now sadly demolished, this small, fun house with its cinema-like tower above the entrance was a prime and early example of *moderne*.

The architect of the Midland Hotel at Morecambe, Oliver Hill, also designed a house on the south coast further towards Poole, but still exploiting the magnificent views of the harbour. Landfall was built for a wealthy amateur film-maker, the 25-year-old Dudley Shaw Ashton and his young family. Described by the present owner as 'champagne socialists', the young couple welcomed guests to the informal atmosphere of their *moderne* home, in a pattern already established for the commissioning of such seaside retreats. Visitors included Oliver Hill, Henry Moore and Ben Nicholson. Ashton wished the ground plan of the house to centre around the construction of a circular room, based on his favourite film clip from *Evergreen* starring Jessie Matthews, in which she plays a grand piano. This circular room or main hall also doubled as a film theatre, with a retractable screen and built-in projection facilities. The Danish beechwood floor extended into the adjacent living-room, both spaces being decorated with Marion Dorn rugs. The two rooms could be joined into one for entertaining by folding back the dividing doors (Figure 36). The living-room was south-facing, with sliding glass doors on to the terrace outside with its external, ship-style staircase leading to the balcony above. This saved children with sandy feet tramping through the house, allowing them to walk straight to their bathroom. The interior staircase led off the hall and swept upwards, complete with rope handrail; the wall beside it is punctuated by porthole-shaped windows. The house generated a feeling of moving through fluid space, not dissimilar to the experience of walking through a Le Corbusier house of the same period. The stairs led again on to the roof-top sun room and terrace. The house was furnished with Betty Joel furniture in blond woods, paid for by the symbolic gesture of the Ashtons' selling their antique family furniture and buying new from the queen of *moderne* design. The house is well preserved by its enthusiastic present owners. The use of colour by Oliver Hill is significant. Often, architecture of the 1930s such as this is seen only by means of black- and-white photographs and films. However, the use of colour was important and varied. The Critall metal window frames were painted leaf green, the balcony pale salmon and the doors pale yellow. With the house set amidst pine trees with the terrace and smooth lawn stretching southwards, the feeling is very much of divisions between interior and exterior melting away, of sun terraces, open-air balconies and lots of light.

Adventurous use of colour was a keynote of the *moderne* dwelling. 'Torilla' at Hatfield in Hertfordshire was a two-storey, square house with flat roof built in 1935. The reinforced concrete of its exterior was painted pale pink. The metal window frames for these houses were invariably painted green, as in a house at Farnborough, Kent designed by Oswald Milne in 1936 and one at Beeston Regis, Norfolk in 1934, which also had emerald green doors. Designed by the same architect, W. F. Tuthill, is a house at Aylmerton, also in Norfolk. The geometric lines of this two-storey house are enhanced by cream rendering, accentuated by the orange windows and door, the bright red columns of the balcony and verandah and the cerulean blue railings. The decorative shutters that frame the windows were painted in orange and ivory zigzag lines

Figure 36 Oliver Hill, Landfall, Poole Harbour

and the exterior colour scheme of orange and yellow was originally continued into the interior, with all fittings installed in chromium steel. 'The Uplands' (1935) at Blythe Bridge, Staffordshire even had orange drainpipes to complement the green windows.

The use of colour in the interior was also a prevalent theme during the 1930s, with advice on decoration appearing in book form. *The Studio Yearbook of Decorative Arts* began to carry colour plates, and three key books were published. Derek Patmore's *Colour Schemes for the Modern Home* (1933) was illustrated with 24 colour photographs of professionally decorated domestic interiors. The interior decorator Basil Ionides wrote *Colour and Interior Decoration* (1926) and *Colour in Everyday Rooms* (1934), both published by *Country Life*. In *Colour in Everyday Rooms* Ionides recommended the use of glossy surfaces to brighten up dark rooms. Gloss paint, gold or silver leaf or mirrors were recommended. A further tip was to fit the window sill with a mirror: 'Not an ordinary silver mirror, as this would throw grey lights on to the ceiling, but with a pink tinted, or, better still, a gold-leaf mirror. The gold-leaf-mirror will throw most beautiful sunlight effects upwards on the dullest of days, and will cheer up the gloomiest of rooms' (1934: 38). The use of lighting in the interior also exercised Ionides, as electricity had made a variety of lighting in one room a possibility for the first time. There was also no need to take ventilation into consideration, as had been the case with gas or oil in the past. In one example, a modest-sized bedroom is lit by two lozenge-shaped wall lights above a mirrored fireplace, one ceiling light with five separate bulbs and two separate concealed lights above the twin beds, which backed on to a mirrored wall (Figure 37).

Moderne houses were therefore distinguished by their all-white or cream exteriors with jewel-like colours as accents. There was almost always a sun-terrace, veranda and/or balcony designed as part of the house. The situation was usually suburban or near the beach. The patrons were usually wealthy young people who wanted to leave behind the formality of their Edwardian upbringing. But these were one-off, specially commissioned houses. *Moderne* houses were also built by speculative builders in the less select suburban areas such as Kingston, Colindale and Hendon. Connected by means of the new underground railway routes as well as the road network, these suburban areas of London boomed. The term *moderne* was even used to sell semi-detached houses featuring curved bay windows with metal frames, streamlined horizontal stripes and flat roofs. The architect Herbert Welch, designer of the first 'Suntrap' estate in Edgware in 1932, used *moderne* design to distinguish his work. A brochure entitled 'Haymills Moderne Houses' of the 1930s used the *moderne* term as a promotional device. The *moderne* style also lent itself to the design of multi-storey blocks of flats or apartments. Gwynne House in Turner Street, London, has a flat roof and curved balconies, and was painted pink with black window frames. There were also more up-market examples, including Marshall and Tweedy's Viceroy Court, NW1 and some privately built flats outside London, even as far north as Moor Court, overlooking the Town Moor in the north of Newcastle. My father worked for Marshall and Tweedy, a Newcastle firm of architects, in the early 1960s. They had designed a number of offices in Newcastle in very staid, classical style. However, their own office, now demolished, was built just before the war in *moderne* style. They also used luscious materials such as chrome, imported marble and terrazzo in their other *moderne* work, such as Carrick's tea houses in Newcastle.

The Feminized Interior

No large-scale residence was commissioned in pure *moderne* style in Britain. The *moderne* and glamour were associated with femininity and

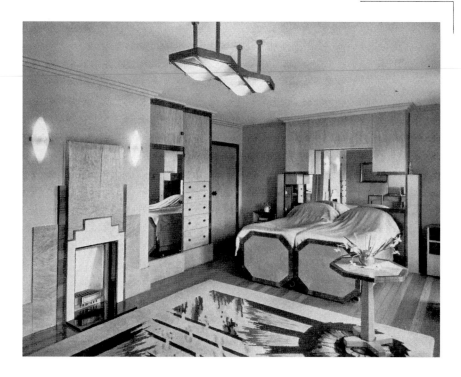

Figure 37 Basil Ionides, *Colour in Everyday Rooms*, 'A Modern Bedroom', 1934

effeminacy. The style was equated with feminine narcissism and camp, with gazing idly in mirrors or posing against complementary backdrops. The *moderne* was also used for the design of buildings for mass entertainment or shopping, and was thus perceived by the critics as a style catering for the despised lower-middle and working-classes. In complete contrast, Modernism was masculine, radical, pure, strong, heterosexual, elite and overtly politicized. Hence a minority of female aristocratic patrons chose to refurbish their traditionally styled new or inherited homes in a glamorous, Hollywood style, but not using Modernism.

One key example is Lady Edwina Mountbatten. When Lord and Lady Mountbatten travelled to America for their honeymoon in 1922 they scandalized respectable society on both sides of the Atlantic by staying at Pickfair, the home of Mary Pickford and Douglas Fairbanks in Hollywood, and not mingling with New York's high society. Furthermore, they acted in a Charlie Chaplin film with Jackie Cougan and toured the Paramount sets created for *Robin Hood* with Cecil B. De Mille. Their honeymoon photographs show them frolicking in the grounds of Pickfair with Charlie Chaplin and posing by the Grand Canyon in full cowboy and cowgirl gear (Figure 38). Lord Mountbatten remained a lifelong film fan and brought back films, projector and jazz records from Hollywood to show in his own private cinema. The couple travelled to America twice more during the inter-war years and enjoyed a heady lifestyle as part of the Prince of Wales's entourage, but transgressed traditional notions of glamour as defined by aristocracy – they followed the Hollywood lead. The design of the couple's Penthouse, a remodelling of the top two storeys of a Victorian mansion on Park Lane, Mayfair, caused a stir when it was completed in 1937. It was the first American-style penthouse to be created in Britain, and contained the couple's heirlooms and family crests, but also the latest American gadgets and a high-speed lift. It was designed by an American society decorator, Mrs Joshua Cosden. Their home was featured in a broad range of popular publications, including *Woman* (1951), *Country Life* (1939), *The Studio* (1937), and the *Studio Yearbook* (1938). The articles dwelt on the contrasts between the antique and the modern, but also the masculine and feminine spaces of the interior. Lord Mountbatten's study, with its wooden fitted furniture, dark brown carpet, map of the world and pale blue walls was in direct contrast to the cream, white and pale grey furnishings of Lady Mountbatten's glamorous bedroom. Here the chandelier, venetian blind and satin bed cover were the ultimate in luxury and glamour. Lord Mountbatten's study contained modern gadgets, including a radiogram cabinet that housed a wireless, an electric gramophone turntable and a hand-operated turntable. An aluminium loudspeaker was set into the wall above, with space beneath to allow for the storage of 78 r.p.m. records. The bathroom was also Hollywood-inspired, with its huge mirrors and chromed washstand and heated towel rail

The bathroom was frequently the site for *moderne* design, as America was widely regarded as having the best plumbing and most comprehensive sanitary facilities of any country. Evelyn Waugh used the *moderne* style to epitomize the loathsome *nouveau riche* characters, Mrs Beaver and her son John, in *A Handful of Dust* (1934). Mrs Beaver, an interior decorator, uses the foremost American techniques for her clients, including: 'a Canadian lady who was having her walls covered with chromium plating at immense expense'. Mrs Beaver was converting a house in Belgravia into smart flats: 'with limitless hot water and every transatlantic refinement' (Waugh 1988: 56, 42). Oliver Hill's design (1929–32) of the bathroom for Mrs Ashley, who became Lady Mount Temple during the time of the project, was spectacular and influential. It was widely illustrated and reproduced in the most

Figure 38 Lord and Lady Mountbatten on Honeymoon Dressed as Cowboys

fashionable of the mass-circulation, home-style publications such as *Harper's Bazaar* (1931) and *The Queen* (1931), *Country Life* (1932) and the *Sketch* (1932) – even being an early example of colour illustration in *Decorative Art: Yearbook of the Studio* (1936). Lady Mount Temple had a hand in the design and is credited with such in the publications. The room has grey mirrored glass facing on walls and ceiling, and the glossy floor was Belgian black marble. The Empire-style stool had a hidden tray top in which the gold-sprayed stain cushion could be stored and on which Lady Mount Temple could sit to preen herself in front of the mirrored dressing-table. Further Hollywood touches were added, with concealed illuminated strips above the window and wash basin and illuminated panel behind the bath (Figure 39). Paul Nash's design for a bathroom for the Austrian dancer Ottilie (Tilly) Losch shared similar features and was equally renowned. Losch had married wealthy Edward James in 1931, only to find it was not the lavender marriage that she had hoped. (2) The bathroom at Wimpole Street was designed to entrance Tilly Losch to set up home in the London town house. It featured every up-to-date convenience, including electric fire plus dance barre for exercise. The walls were sheathed in dimpled, dark mulberry glass, which contrasted with the strip neon lights on the wall and ceiling.

Waugh's stereotype of the vapid society decorator had resonance during the 1930s and was linked with Americanization. The profession of interior decorator was American-inspired, figures in New York such as Wharton and Elsie de Wolfe laying the foundations of decorating for a living in the early years of the twentieth century. Increased transatlantic travel amongst the upper classes, as was the case with the Mountbattens, brought the practice to Britain during the 1920s. Women like Syrie Maugham and Sybil Colefax then undertook commissions for the decoration of wealthy clients' interiors from the late 1920s onwards. The profession was popularly associated with women or gay men (Massey 1990; McNeil 1994). Most decorators during the 1930s found commissions in revamping the interiors of existing houses for the affluent. Not only did the American model dictate the practice of interior decoration, but it also influenced the look of the designs. The strict modern movement was unpalatable to the majority of such clients at the time, as they did not subscribe to the values represented by modernism. Far better was the muted *moderne*, which took the functional aspects of modernist aesthetic but mingled them with the decorative qualities and touches of glamour seen on the cinema screen. As David Joel, the estranged husband of the *moderne* furniture designer, Betty Joel, recalled of the 1930s: 'The cinema, whether for bad or for good, had become part of the life of the people and was influencing the furnishing of the people's homes. Usually the film showed glamorous interiors, sometimes good examples of the best of the Modern Movement' (1969: 30). In a similar vein, Julia Cairns, writing in *Film Fashionland*, noted: 'today there is an increased tendency for the modern home to become more modern in its furniture and furnishings

Figure 39 Oliver Hill, Lady Mount Temple's Bathroom, 1934

– a tendency, I fancy, which is to some extent the outcome of modern films and modern plays with their appreciation of modern *decor* and modern furniture' (March 1934: 27).

The influence of Hollywood can also be seen in the image of the society photographer Cecil Beaton and the Hon. Stephen Tennant holding copies of *Photoplay* and *Modern Screen* across their faces,

Figure 40 Cecil Beaton and Stephen Tennant at Wilsford Manor, 1938

masquerading as Norma Shearer and Katherine Hepburn. The photograph was taken to mark Beaton's weekend visit to Tennant's country retreat, Wilsford Manor in deepest Wiltshire (Figure 40). Cecil Beaton recorded in his diary from the period, later published as *The Wandering Years*, a weekend visit to Wilsford Manor in the summer of 1937: 'We looked at scrap-books of old photographs and he rhapsodized suitable texts. Some very ordinary photographs of Garbo were brought to life by "rapt ecstasies"' (1961: 316). Tennant revamped his inherited residence, the early twentieth-century Manor, in a more fashionable style, painting the interior panelling white in 1930 and employing Syrie Maugham to redecorate in 1938. Maugham's famous 'White Room' of 1933 was also photographed by Cecil Beaton, complete with his sister in flowing white, bias cut gown reflected in the mirrored panels of the folding screen.

An important designer and manufacturer of *moderne* furniture and interiors was Betty Joel. She did not work for the upmarket clients of Oliver Hill, but the upper middle classes, who could afford her beautifully crafted goods. Her furniture and interiors were always glamorous, and she had continuous contact with the film industry. She designed and produced luscious furniture for British-made films, including *Love and Let Love* with the German *émigré* art director Alfred Junge. As her husband recalled, visitors to their shop at 25 Knightsbridge included Lord and Lady Mountbatten and the musician Sir Arthur Bliss, and 'Stage and screen folk often visited and furnished film sets and play scenes' (1969: 32). Her ideas came from the Parisian avant-garde, Hollywood and yacht-building (Wilk 1995: 8) Betty Joel's first factories had been at Hayling Island and then Portsmouth before she commissioned her own, purpose-built factory at Kingston from the President of the Royal Institute of British Architects (RIBA) and Slade Professor of Fine Art, Professor Goodhart-Rendel. The local skills of yacht-building were incorporated into Joel's designs in the curved shape of the woods and the solid construction of her wardrobes and desks. A lighter, more curvilinear approach began to appear Joel's work after 1930. The solid, square American mahogany of a 1930 dressing-table (Figure 41) can be contrasted with an example from 1935 (Figure 42), in which a circular mirror is flanked on one side by three curved drawers that pivoted out and on the other by three graduated shelves. The dressing-table of 1935 came in dark wood and blonde wood, with black painted trim and chromium-plated, metal handles. The drum-shaped stool that accompanied the dressing table also came with a dark or blonde wood base and black or maroon velvet upholstery. Other examples of glamorous furniture include her Vienna divan with a sycamore plinth, covered in gold satin and featured in *The Studio Yearbook* (1939).

Joel defended the Hollywood touches in her designs against modernist critics. Geoffrey Boumphrey took issue with her approach in *Architectural Review* during 1935. He complained:

It is no good: with the best will in the world I cannot fit Mrs. Joel's work into the framework of ideas which I constructed with such labour in the first six of these articles. Nor has she any wish to be accommodated. But let her speak for herself: 'When you speak of "the masses", I can only reply that in fifteen years of business I have not yet met them. I have only met innumerable individuals trying to please themselves by choosing beautiful things . . . there is room for individual taste and variety and for many different form of self-expression. The question is: who is to decide what is right? What is right for me may very well be all wrong for you . . . the tendency today is to dragoon the "masses" into accepting a bleak uniform "culture" that is no culture' (1935: 205).

Figure 41 Betty Joel Dressing Table, 1930

Figure 42 Betty Joel Dressing Table, 1935

Boumphrey made the usual modern movement reply when considering popular taste: 'The masses are those who take their ideas ready-made instead of working them out for themselves. It is therefore worthwhile trying to ensure that the ideas they take shall be reasonably sound ones – even though it lay one open to the charge of dragooning' (1935: 205). Joel's response by letter was published in January 1936, and accused Boumphrey of being a snob. 'There is, in fact, no one who takes his ideas more ready-made than the intellectual snob who treasures his membership of some esoteric clique because it saves him the pain of thinking for himself' (1936: 49). This echoes a view she had voiced during the same year in 'A House and A Home' for the collection, *The Conquest of Ugliness*, published as part of the *British Art in Industry* exhibition with an introduction by the fashionable Prince of Wales. Joel argued:

> It is quite wrong to sneer at mass-production. Half the time this is sheer snobbery. If a person who was making a home were to go to Woolworth's, provided that she chose only the things that she herself really liked, she would be able to collect many excellent articles which would help her to make an *ensemble* which expressed her personality and consequently would satisfy not only herself but her real friends as well (1935: 95).

This is a fascinating exchange of views, as it crystallizes the distinctions first drawn up in the beginning of this chapter. Boumphrey is defending the modernist masculine position, as spelled out in the writing of design critics such as Nikolaus Pevsner and Herbert Read. Such critics believed that modern design could radically change society. The masses did not understand modernism, but it was the critics' duty to convince them by means of BBC radio, *The Listener* and new Pelican paperbacks that this was the way forward to a brighter future. Designers such as Joel and Oliver Hill disagreed. While modernist critics characterized them as pandering to popular taste and the vulgar, these designers were far more successful in expressing the values and qualities of modernity than the modern movement itself. Their success came partly from the work that Hollywood cinema had done in presenting attractive decoration and design on the screen. Many of the *moderne* designers contributed to the *Exhibition of British Art in Industry* held at the Royal Academy during January to March 1935. Joel supplied the bedroom suite in Queensland walnut and maple for a specimen bedroom designed by H. C. Bradshaw. Here again were the curved dressing-table, stool and curved bed to match. Oliver Hill designed another glamorous bathroom using glass. The bathroom suite was in lilac porcelain and vitreous china, with chromium-plated metal fittings. The floor, walls and ceiling were decorated with grey silver plate glass.

The glitz and glamour of satin, chrome and reflective glass were anathema to the modernists, who berated the exhibition. However, the work of designers like Joel and Hill fed in to and was part of the broader popularity of the *moderne*. If clients could not afford to shop at Joel's Knightsbridge showroom or commission Hill to design for them, then they could emulate the look by reference to popular magazines and by watching Hollywood films. The most ubiquitous feature of the *moderne* interior, and the cheapest and easiest to copy, as seen on the screen and in magazines, was the satin bed cover. Wealthy patrons like Lady Edwina Mountbatten, more mid-range bedrooms featured in *The Studio* and recollections of working-class bedrooms of the 1930s attest to the popularity of the shiny bed cover. Used to great effect in Hollywood films, notably *Dinner at Eight,* it was translated into satin for Lady Edwina Mountbatten and mass-produced in synthetic fabrics, most likely rayon, for the working-class home. The synthetic bedspreads came in brilliant shades of gold, burgundy, sapphire blue or emerald green. They provided an affordable touch of glamour in a room that had previously received little attention, apart from in the homes of the very rich. The bedspread would cover the worn sheets and blankets beneath and provide a little flight of fancy, away from the reality of being so cold that coats and even door mats were placed on beds to keep the incumbents warm (Interview with author 1998). The bedspreads did not add extra warmth and so were not strictly functional: they were significant in representing fantasy and desire in the bedroom. The mass-circulation magazines provided ideas for emulating the luxury of the stars' bedrooms. In *Film Fashionland* June 1934 'Bedroom Secrets' were revealed by Julia Cairns, and the beds of Norma Shearer, Lelia Hyams and Jeanette MacDonald were illustrated. It was suggested that the satin bedspread of Norma Shearer could be easily copied: 'Doesn't it make your fingers itch to make one like it? It is in natural coloured pongee (a thin plain-weave silk fabric, usually from India or China) embroidered in spare moments!' (1934: 34). Indeed, do-it-yourself tips frequently graced the pages of the fan magazines. *Film Fashionland* advised in 1934 when discussing colour: 'Now, there isn't the slightest reason why you shouldn't play this same little trick in your home. . . . Find a corner cupboard (one in unpainted hardwood would be inexpensive). Paint the outside brown, the inside soft honey-yellow; then bring out that cheery modern china. Let this Bing Crosby colour trick croon sweetly in your home' (1934: 33).

The dressing-table was another feature to enjoy popularity during the 1930s. This was a comparatively new type of furniture for the bedroom, as *The Queen* review of Betty Joel's 'Token' dressing table from 1923 reveals: 'A dwarf dressing table, at which one can sit comfortably on a low stool in front of a tall mirror, with brushes and toilet accessories literally under one's hand, is a modern development in furnishing, that certainly spells the last word in comfort. Such a desirable possession is Betty Joel's "Token" Vanity Set' (6 December 1923: as quoted *in Designs by Betty Joel of Token*, 1927: 4). The dressing-table frequently featured in Hollywood films, providing an ideal moment for narcissistic reflection on the part of the heroine, usually reflecting on the errors of her ways or scheming ahead, as seen again in *Dinner at Eight*. Hollywood films helped to popularize the dressing-table. When the homes of female Hollywood stars were featured in magazines, there was usually a photograph and a discussion of her dressing-table as the symbol of modern femininity. The home of Lilian Harvey featured in *Film Fashionland* in 1934, including her 'sensibly designed dressing-table with its "petticoat" matching the curtains. This, like the pelmet, is edged with a deeper green silk braid. The plate-glass top gives a pleasant modern finish and reflects its charming accessories in soft blues, with cream table-lights shaded in petal-pink' (April 1934: 25). Carole Lombard's home and dressing-table came up for scrutiny in the June issue of *Film Fashionland*. 'Very feminine, very modern, the dressing-room – one mirror wall, the others "off-white" with built-in wardrobes to match. Frivolous black lace window drapes, a flounced rose stool and a glass-topped dressing-table are interesting features' (1934: 32). The woman at the dressing-table was also a recurring image in magazine advertising and illustrations for features of the 1930s. *Hall's Wine*, a special tonic and pick-me-up, had been on the market since the nineteenth century. However, adverts of the 1930s show a silhouette of a woman slumped on an easy chair whilst an idealized, Hollywood figure stands in full evening gown looking happily into a hand-held mirror standing before a dressing-table. 'Rise out of that miserable cold-weakened self' urges the advert, revealing that the perfect, revitalized self is to be found by looking into the mirror.

Bedroom suites were manufactured for the middle-class and working-class markets, and different decorations sold. In 1936, for example, the mid-range, south London department store Arding and Hobbs advertised bedroom suites in the local newspapers. These came in traditional styles or *moderne*, and consisted of a lady's wardrobe, a smaller gentleman's wardrobe and a dressing-table. There were also options to buy matching bedstead, breakfast table, slipper box and bedside cupboard. 'Convenient payments' were also offered to allow the costs to spread over 12, 24 or 36 months, and prices ranged from 24 to 28 guineas. Glass trays, glass powder bowl and powder puff, a metal-backed hairbrush, small containers in pink glass with chrome lids and scent bottles with attached bulbs were used in the adverts to adorn the dressing-tables and bought by women to decorate their glamorous territory. All dressing-tables carried triple mirrors to enable all-round views of the head. Home- made, finely crocheted doilies or embroidered mats might complete the dressing table set. During the early 1950s when my father was studying to become an architect in Newcastle he: 'was taught to deride people who had dressing-tables and placed them in the bay windows of the "accursed semi"' (In interview with aut 1998).

The other aspect of the new era of modernity to affect the majority of homes, regardless of class, was the radio. In the designer home, radios were housed in built-in cabinets to blend in with the rest of the *moderne* furnishings. At Landfall House a special cabinet was constructed out of cedar to house the radiogram and cocktail cabinet in order to match the other built-in cupboards and shelves. The less wealthy consumer might buy the Kolster-Brandes (KB) radio as designed and advertised by Betty Joel in the mid-1930s. The cabinet was solid in construction, with a recess in which to store books at the base. It was made from Queensland walnut and chrome, with simple-to-use dials and rounded corners. Like other symbols of modernity, for example cars and aeroplanes, no prototypes existed for radio cabinets, so designers either tried to borrow styles from the past to encase the machinery or, more commonly, adopted the *moderne* as the acceptable symbol of new technology. By featuring Betty Joel in the adverts the manufacturers were alluding to radio's ease of use and up-to-date stylishness. Manufacturers were aware that women made the majority of purchasing decisions for the home, and so new technology for the domestic setting was designed for the female consumer. This was based on certain stereotypes, as an official representative of the 1932 Radio Exhibition at Olympia commented:

> Women are not technically minded and manufacturers have, during the past year, gone out of their way to cater for women by two methods. First, they have reduced the operation of a radio set to the utmost simplicity; in many cases the turning of one switch only is required. There are also several automatic tuning devices which make the act of tuning purely mechanical, and require no special knowledge. The other

way in which woman has been catered for is by constructing radio set
cabinets of such design and character as to have a definite feminine appeal
(20 August 1932).

The feminization of the design of many new electrical products, from
ovens to vacuum cleaners, characterized the period. Just as women were
encouraged to decorate their homes through an appeal to supposed
feminine narcissism, so too they were urged to follow Hollywood in
decorating themselves in front of the new dressing-table mirror.

Putting On The Style

A revolution in beauty and cosmetics took place in the 1930s, thanks
again to Hollywood. Make-up became socially acceptable and widely
available for the first time. It was associated with being glamorous, as
an editorial piece in *Home Chat* (1939) demonstrates. 'That Touch of
Glamour' advised readers on the application of make-up, including
rouge, eye-shadow and lip pencil. Max Factor of Hollywood was the
leading brand of beauty products in Britain, and was marketed there
from 1930 onwards, with the London Salon opening in February 1937.
Elizabeth Arden, although she had never produced make-up for use
during actual filming, did advise women in 1934 to: 'Hitch Your Beauty
to a Star' in *Film Fashionland*: 'It's fun to have a new face, to be exotic
in one's new trained evening gown, "out of door" in tweeds, and
demure in a "little" dress. . . . Round faces can be made to look oval,
thin one plumper. These are clever little tricks that are not reserved for
stage and screen folk, but you and I can copy' (March 1934: 23). The
advertising for such products used the *moderne* vocabulary, with the
same swept-back lines, and incorporated literal references to Hollywood
and Hollywood stars with the introduction of celebrity endorsements
in 1930. It was not only Max Factor that used star endorsements;
products like Icilma Peach Powder featured Universal Pictures star Gloria
Stuart. The scope for emulation of Hollywood stars by means of beauty
products was used by *Amami* henna shampoos during the 1930s. In
1936 an advert in *Home Chat* read 'Is this Jean Harlow? No! This
attractive young lady is Kay Dillon of London – another Amami lovely!'
The lettering can be described as elongated in form and asymmetrical,
quite unlike its art deco or Bauhaus contemporaries.

A sample of adverts from women's magazines of the 1930s also reveals
the extent to which the British aristocracy was still an important a
source of fashionability, almost as important as the Hollywood stars.

Pond's Face Powder was endorsed in a run of adverts by Lady Ursula Stewart, Lady Marguerite Strickland, Lady Milbanke, Lady Barbara Gore and Viscountess Moore. California Poppy perfume enjoyed the endorsement of Lady Moira Combe and the Countess of Carlisle. What is interesting about the two campaigns is that the portraits of the women are based on Hollywood prototypes, to judge by the use of lighting, profiles and clothing. Discussion of presentations at court, foreign royal families, births, deaths and marriages and visits to the races also featured on the pages of a mass-circulation magazine like *Home Chat*. It was often the glamorous clothes of the aristocrats that occupied the magazine. In April 1936 readers were presented with a portrait of the Countesse de Crayamel, younger daughter of shipowner Sir John Latta, with the caption: 'The very lovely person below in the glorious silver fox cape (doesn't it make you sigh with envy?) . . .'. My mother recalls that sources of fashion came not only from Hollywood but also from the British aristocracy as glimpsed in the pages of *The Tatler*, which her father bought occasionally as a treat, particularly at Christmas, when a colourful bumper version was sold (In interview with author 1998)

Hollywood fashions were highly influential, and British women were able to emulate them, adapting them to their own requirements and taste if necessary through home dressmaking. *Home Chat* featured clothes from Hollywood films and illustrated sources for paper patterns. On 1 January 1938 there was a photograph of Marlene Dietrich in a full-length evening gown featured in the film *Angel*, with examples of Bestway Patterns that could be bought and a dress that could be made to emulate the look. However, this was not straightforward copying: women were advised about the types of fabric suitable for such a gown, but the choice was definitely left to them. There was even a short-lived magazine devoted solely to Hollywood fashion. *Film Fashionland* began publication in March 1934 under the strap-line of : 'The Charm of the Film World Brought to Every Woman's Life'. Priced at 6d, it was three times as expensive as *Home Chat* and was beautifully produced, with heavier quality paper and colour illustrations. The magazine came with a free pattern in every monthly issue, the first being for a shirt and skirt modelled on the cover by Fox Film star, Miriam Jordan. Further paper patterns could be ordered from the magazine, based on examples worn by Hollywood stars. The magazine carried adverts that featured other brands of patterns and recommendations for fabric. In July 1934 Horrocks, the textile manufacturers, advertised their piqué voile dress, as worn by British film star Dorothy Hyson. 'Nothing Difficult About This Charming Film Frock – You Can Make It For A Few Shillings' ran the copy. For the more affluent woman, dresses could be bought ready-made from major department stores like D. H. Evans and Parnell's in London or by mail order.

In addition to the plethora of ways in which Hollywood affected everybody's lives in 1930s Britain in the form of fashion, interior décor and make-up, it also affected those growing up in the Hollywood era. As American film grew in respectability as the 1930s progressed, so the movies appealed more and more to children. The appeal of Shirley Temple meant that my mother was very nearly christened Shirley instead of Gwendoline. My father also recalls: 'Spin-offs – children were named after film stars. My brother Raymond Massey. There were Shirleys, Deannas, etc.' (In interview with author 1998). Children were also trained to dance like Shirley Temple: 'Young Girls learned to tap dance – Miss Madison's in Consett where my cousin Doreen – a lookalike Shirley Temple – tapped away in front of local audience' (In interview with author 1998). Special children's Saturday matinées also became popular during the 1930s. It was not only seeing the films but the stars in the flesh that remained in my father's memory: 'In my time my mother took me to Newcastle frequently to see shows or music hall (variety acts they were called). Many of the film stars appeared. As a young boy I particularly remember the "cowboy" Tom Mix with his white horse and cowboy gang. Also Alan Jones who was famous for singing "Donkey Serenade" on a film' (In interview with author 1998).

The *moderne* style was all-pervasive during the 1930s in Britain. It was used for the design of virtually all building types and their interiors, including hotels, houses, flats, factories, shops, garages, airports, railway stations, golf club-houses, cinemas and offices in almost every town and city. It inspired aspects of transport design, fashion, furniture, advertising, film-set design and beauty products. The word itself did have meaning in Britain at the time: for instance, the *Moderne* cinema was built in Winton near Bournemouth, Dorset in 1935. The opening of the cinema was only mentioned in the local newspaper, *The Times and Directory*, which gives a useful contemporary definition of the word:

> The '*Moderne*' Cinema fully justifies its name. It is, indeed, the last word in the modernistic style of building and architecture. Externally, of course, the main building has no special features and is, in fact, almost unnotice-able from the main Wimborne Road, bur the brilliantly lighted entrance from which a wide corridor leads to the main hall, is an attractive feature. Inside the visitor cannot fail to be pleasantly surprised by the luxurious atmosphere of comfort which is conveyed by the very simplicity of the

furnishing. This may seems a paradox, but in conformity with the modern taste the fittings, in which chromium plays a large part, have an illusive attraction which contrasts with the former vogue of elaborate ornamentation. The new type of interior decoration produces a pleasing effect of plastic design. The most novel feature is the streamline shape of the auditorium and the grilled effect of concealed lighting.

The glamour of Hollywood through the allure of the *moderne* had a huge impact on both sides of the Atlantic during the 1930s. Glamour was equated with modernity and an American lifestyle. This provoked the British elite to retaliate with acts of parliament restricting the exhibition of American films and an intellectual elite who used the terms 'jazz' and 'Hollywood' to denote what they regarded as inferior design aimed at the masses. The fond hope was that the masses would wake up and realise the intrinsic value of British cinema and Modernist design, which they did not.

Notes

1. *Grand Hotel* is the only film where Garbo utters the lines: 'I want to be alone.'
2. The couple lived apart from December 1931. James financed two ballets as showcases for Tilly's talents in 1933, but the marriage ended with a messy divorce. Tilly filed for divorce but James counterfiled, naming Prince Serge Obolensky as the third party. James was then shunned by upper-class society.

Cold War Cultures: Hollywood and Modernism

The popularity of Hollywood continued unabated in Britain throughout the Second World War up until the mid-1960s. American hegemony was then challenged in style terms by the ascendancy of British culture as the source of glamour and modernity, in which film played an important part. The battle for cultural control outlined in Chapters 1 and 2 continued, played out during the war by official British documentary-style propaganda competing with films like the glamorous saga *Gone With the Wind* (1939) and the dazzling *Babes on Broadway* (1942). After the war British authorities renewed attempts to compete with the power of American popular culture by establishing various official bodies to police everyday culture. Competition for Hollywood films in the US and Britain came from television. Hollywood retaliated with widescreen, smellovision, technicolor and action-packed musicals and Westerns. Viewers were no longer as impressed by the luscious décor of cinemas as homes became more comfortable; what attracted them was the spectacle unfolding on the screen itself. The *moderne* was a dated style, although still in evidence during the 1940s and early 1950s. What emerged as part of America's increased presence as a world power was that modernism was reinvented to represent American values of democracy and liberalism during the 1950s. Hence, artists and designers who had struggled during the 1930s now found recognition and lucrative commissions, even from official sources, in the name of the Cold War. Unofficial Cold War culture also made an impact in Britain through Hollywood, particularly for the new, teenage audience and through the increased fragmentation of the audience.

British National Identity and Hollywood Glamour at War

The British film industry, beleaguered since the 1920s and 1930s by the challenge of American popular films, had enjoyed limited artistic success in terms of its documentary films, led by the film-maker John Grierson. The documentary film movement had produced short corporate films for official organizations, including the Empire Marketing Board Film Unit, the General Post Office Film Unit, the BBC and the British Coke and Gas Company (Higson in Barr (ed.) 1986). This was channelled in to the official war efforts from 1939 onwards to inform and influence the British public under the auspices of the Ministry of Information's Films Division and government guidelines for commercial producers. Production space was limited, and only one-third of the pre-war quantities of British films were made, approximately sixty feature films annually (Street 1997: 11). Examples include *Target for Tonight* (1941) and *Fires Were Started* (1943), which drew upon the British documentary tradition of representing everyday life in realist style. Fashion and glamour were not a central part of these worthy documentaries. As Pam Cook has argued: 'One important consequence of the anti-Hollywood position was the central part played in the consensus films by de-glamorised British heroines, whose down-to-earth ordinariness was depicted as essential to national unity' (1996: 30). The challenge of a sexually charged, feminine glamour was not considered appropriate to the construction of a British national identity during the Second World War. The entry of women into the male working environment was certainly a feature of wartime propaganda; but the challenge to accepted morality and the threat to family unity that the war engendered was not a feature of British films of this period.

Hollywood films such as the Oscar winning *Mrs Miniver* (1942), set in wartime Britain, were immensely popular and helped boost morale through the restrained use of glamour. This MGM production, which presented a fictionalized account of a British family's survival during the war, was the top box draw for 1942 according to *Kinematograph Weekly*'s annual survey (Lant 1991: 231). The film was based on the 'Mrs Miniver' column, which appeared in *The Times* during the late 1930s. The picture hat with veil worn by Greer Garson as Kay Miniver inspired women in Britain to wear the same during times of rationing, attempting to emulate the star and maintain a glamorous image when there were severe restrictions on the production and purchase of clothing through the Utility scheme. As Mrs Allen, a participant in the *York History Project*, recalled: 'The girls used to copy the hats because hats were really in then in films. Veils over the faces you know' (1988: 69).

The US did not enter the war until 1942, and even then Hollywood's film production remained almost at the same level, although there were restrictions in terms of location shooting in the US. In *Home Chat* of 24 August 1940, readers were advised: 'For momentary forgetfulness of War – and War-time worries – Filmland brings you entertainment grim and glamorous' (p. 12). In the 4 November 1939 issue, readers could: 'go and forget your worries by seeing *It's a Wonderful World*' (p. 219). Therefore throughout the war Hollywood remained the main source of popular mass entertainment. The worthy aspirations of the British documentary tradition, played out in terms of a British realist school of film-making during the war, did not aim to compete in terms of glamour and attraction for mass audience popularity. Glamour was perceived to be an anachronism during the ravages of wartime experiences of bombing and the disintegration of the family unit. The main exception to this were the costume dramas of Gainsborough Studios of 1943–50. Eschewed by the British film establishment at the time and critically neglected until recently, the films presented drama rather than documentary in period settings (Harper 1994). Films such as *The Man in Grey* (1943) and *Fanny By Gaslight* (1944) were the top box office successes of the year, particularly attracting female cinemagoers (Lant 1991: 231). However, it was argued that a successful British film industry could not be based on trivial, female glamour. As Evelyn Russell pleaded in 'Why Not a School of British Film-Making?' in *Sight and Sound*: 'no anachronisms . . . no box office glamour . . . and no loose ends' (1941: 12). Antonia Lant has argued that British film-makers, critics and producers regarded the war as an opportunity to create a successful national cinema in the service of the war effort that would be liberated from the hegemony of Hollywood: 'Good, convincing acting was a plus, while imitation of Hollywood glamour was to be avoided, for glamour and convincing acting were understood to be mutually exclusive. It was mental rather than physical polish and slickness that was required' (1991: 33). Sadly for the British film establishment, the majority of British picturegoers still preferred the glamorous offerings of Hollywood before, during and for some time after the Second World War, as my mother's recollections demonstrate.

My mother's family moved to Tow Law in County Durham during the war, as my grandfather was given the job of key man, responsible for training other workers in the foundry side of arms production for

Vickers Armstrong. He was in charge of the steam drop hammer and worked twelve-hour shifts daily. The family was moved into an old vicarage, which was so spacious that another family were moved in with them. There was a cinema at Tow Law with Saturday morning programmes for children: Westerns with Roy Rogers and Laurel and Hardy comedies. Admission was often by means of presenting a used jam jar. In the evenings she went to see romances with her mother. The cinema was very basic; they once noticed a strange smell in the cinema and discovered there was a dead rat under the floorboards.[1] Cinema was a crucial part of surviving the war. As my mother recalls: 'During the war people turned to Hollywood as an escape from war and rationing. My mother was keen on Hollywood. A lot of women were because they were very difficult times to live through, and if you didn't have some sort of release or dream it was hard. There was some horrible things happening, bombs were dropping and you had to go in the air raid shelters, things like that. People were being killed. Watching the news was horrible. You wanted to get away from it. It touched everyone' (In interview with author 1998).

One key romantic film of the Second World War was *Now, Voyager* (1942), starring Bette Davis, recently described by the middle-brow newspaper, *The Independent,* as: 'dreadful, of course, which is what makes this legendary Bette Davis tear-jerker such a kitsch classic' (9 December 1998, p. 18). However, the narrative, reinforced by the set design and art direction, sees a dowdy Charlotte Vane (Bette Davies) trapped in the austere, nineteenth-century décor of her overbearing mother's Boston mansion. She escapes by means of psychiatric treatment and a cruise. The transformation is represented through her shaped and plucked eyebrows, weight loss, a new coiffure and a glamorous wardrobe. Upon her return Charlotte's mother attempts to force her into the clothes she wore as the repressed daughter, but the new independent Charlotte refuses. Although she falls in love with a married man, a compromise is reached when she takes in his own unwanted teenage daughter, and a compromise relationship is reached. The film ends with her famous line: 'Oh Jerry, don't lets ask for the moon – we have the stars.' The storyline of make-do love, set against the backdrop of luxury New England glamour and a South American cruise, must have had resonance for a wartime audience because of its very poignancy and its very remoteness and glamour. As one woman recalled of the film in 1944: 'I've just seen Bette Davis's film *Now Voyager*, and what enjoyment, what relief – *no war.* I have worked in a large office with other women in whose homes the war is ever present by the absence of husbands and sons on service, and who, like myself, snatch their bit of break in a couple of hours each week in the cinema' (as quoted in Calder 1969: 427). Whereas women were not presented as sexual beings in British wartime films, the makeover of Charlotte has deliberately erotic overtones (Doane 1987: 39–42).

Post-War Film and Television

Post-war British film production, like other aspects of British post-war culture, built on the experience of producing a consensual national identity during the war. This tendency in British film was epitomized by Ealing productions, which flourished during the early 1950s, with their portrayal of a cosy, middle-class southern English community – much like the Ealing Studios themselves (Barr 1977). For example, *Passport To Pimlico* (1949) and *The Titfield Thunderbolt* (1952) revelled in the warmth of the ties in the local community and dealt with outside threats effectively. Hints of a disturbing, psychological/sexual presence had begun to surface at Ealing, for example in the work of Robert Hamer, *It Always Rains on Sunday* (1947) and *Kind Hearts and Coronets* (1949). However, most represented a rather dowdy, realist rendition of the British way of life set in contemporary times. More challenging were the works of British film-makers Powell and Pressburger, including *A Matter of Life and Death* (1946) and *Red Shoes* (1948), which were outside this reassuring, realist tradition and dealt, in full colour, with themes of sexuality and desire. However, they did not offer available glamour for emulation, as Hollywood films of the same period did.

   Challenged by the popularity of television, Hollywood strove to create greater spectacles for enlarged cinema screens. The British cinema attendance peaked in 1946 with 31.4 million visits per week, but then entered a steady decline, with 25.2 million weekly visits in 1952 and 9.6 million by 1960 (Hiley 1999: 46). One of the most popular and the most spectacular American genres of the post-war era was the Hollywood musical. Television had made an impact earlier in America, and so the industry responded to the threat with the production of fuller-colour, wide-screen extravaganzas. Colour was gradually introduced during the 1940s and 1950s, although not universal until the 1960s (Bordwell, Staiger and Thompson 1988). CinemaScope was introduced in 1953, beginning with *The Robe* and *How To Marry A Millionaire*. This involved using an anamorphic lens that widened the image and gave the impression of three dimensions. Other methods for projecting the film in wider format followed, in the form of VistaVision in 1954 and

Todd-AO in 1955. My mother recalled spectacular musicals like *An American in Paris* (1951), *Seven Brides for Seven Brothers* (1954), *Oklahoma* (1955) (the first film to be produced in Todd-AO), and *Carousel* (1956) and *The King and I* (1956) (the first two films to be produced using the improved CinemaScope 55 process) as the most enjoyable and popular after the war. The huge images on the spectacular screen and improved sound systems were fantastic compared to the variety shows on offer in Newcastle at the time. *An American in Paris* was one of MGM's first colour productions; designed by Cedric Gibbons, it won an Oscar for Best Film. The lavish sets and complex dance routines of Gene Kelly were far more attractive and alluring than the worthy displays of Ealing Cinema. When glamorous British stars were created and enjoyed popular acceptance, as was the case with Diana Dors, she emulated an established Hollywood ideal of the attractive and available woman. In both *Good Time Girl* (1948) and *Dance Hall* (1950) she represented the Rank Charm School's bad girl (Street 1997: 134–5).[2]

Beyond the musical other American genres that exploited special effects to increase their impact included *film noir*, science fiction and horror, which dominated British cinema screens during the 1950s. Apart from films created for the mainstream, a new type of film made for a younger audience had a major impact in Britain and on definitions of glamour for the teenager. For example, *The Wild One* (1953), starring Marlon Brando, was based on a real-life but exaggerated event when a gang of motorcyclists invaded the small town of Hollister on 4 July 1947. The same sense of post-war teenage alienation was portrayed in *East of Eden* (1954) and *Rebel Without A Cause* (1955), both starring James Dean, and *Rock Around the Clock*, released in Britain in 1956. Further examples of youthful rebellion included Elvis Presley in *Jailhouse Rock* – the continued presence and popularity of Hollywood was a problem for the British authorities, who sustained pre-war attempts to control the exhibition of American film and groom a home-grown industry. This was marginally successful during the following decade, when London became the centre of youth fashion and glamour, overshadowing Hollywood for a brief window of time.

The cultural leadership of glamour passed briefly to Britain during the mid- 1960s. This leadership was reinforced by popular film and reworked American themes of teenage rebellion and black music. For example, the figure of government secret agent James Bond underwent an important shift in meaning from the 1950s to the 1960s. When Ian Fleming's novels were first published and serialized in the 1950s he was constructed as a Cold War hero. The *Daily Express* ran extracts of

From Russia with Love in 1957, when his struggles with the shady powers of communism behind the iron curtain were fully dramatized. The first James Bond film, *Dr. No*, was released in 1961, when the Cold War scenario was still dominant. However, the heterosexual interest of the Bond figure also formed an important part of the narrative with Ursula Andress emerging from the sea like a Renaissance Venus, in a daring bikini. By the mid-1960s interviews with Sean Connery in men's magazines, particularly *Playboy*, constructed him as the hero of a new cultural revolution in Britain. As Tony Bennett has argued: 'The Cold War inscription that was dominant in the 1950s, for example, rapidly gave way, in the early 1960s, to Bond's inscription within a new discourse of modernity as the most prominent fictional embodiment of a new image of cultural and political leadership constructed by the media's projection of a rising generation of public figures as a new talent-based, classless, untraditional, anti-Establishment elite destined to lead Britain into the modern age' (1982: 13). The glamour of the James Bond figure appealed particularly to young males. The British toy manufacturer, Dinky, produced its best-seller James Bond car with bullet-proof window shield, ejector seat, revolving number plates and retractable guns at the front. A popular set of bubblegum cards were also bought, collected and swapped avidly by schoolboys. The films also influenced clothing and behaviour: when my husband first travelled on his own at the age of 16 he bought Kent cigarettes to mimic his hero, James Bond. The suavely dressed Bond, driving around glamorous European locations in his Aston Martin DB5, was a great fantasy figure for an apprentice fitter. The clothing worn by Bond, hand-made shoes and dinner jackets, was a stark contrast to the male working-class reality of early British 1960s realist cinema, including *Saturday Night and Sunday Morning* (1960).

A new powerful and sexually charged feminine identity was constructed in a new wave of British cinema that began to make an impact from the early 1960s with films such as *A Taste of Honey* (1961). As Christine Geraghty has argued, changing social mores, particularly exemplified by the Profumo affair and the subsequent Denning Report of 1963, acknowledged the sexual power of young women, in this case to cause the demise of a cabinet minister (1997). British films such as *Darling* (1964) and *Here We Go Round The Mulberry Bush* (1967) centred around the lives of young, sexually attractive women as consumers in the heady context of Swinging London. This image was reinforced by the popularity of The Beatles on both sides of the Atlantic. Their first film, *A Hard Day's Night*, was released in 1964. Its black-and-white form and mix of documentary and fiction directed by Dick Lester was distinctive at the time. I remember seeing it upon release in Newcastle and feeling excited by the sheer cheek and irreverence of the four long-haired, working-class lads.

This image of London as the centre of young glamour, underpinned by a new sense of powerful, female sexuality, was to also permeate popular television series, particularly 'The Avengers'. Produced during 1961–1969, it is recorded as the 'highest grossing British television export ever', broadcast in 120 countries (T. Miller 1997: 5). The fantasy spy series was immensely popular in Britain, spending 103 weeks in the Top Twenty series between the years of its production. The sexual tension lay between Patrick MacNee as John Steed in the British upper-class, traditional male dress of black bowler hat, rolled-up umbrella and three-piece suit with camel overcoat and the direct contrast of the black leather and fetishist-inspired clothing of his female partners, played by Honor Blackman and then Diana Rigg. The hint of black leather and sado-masochism again reinforced the sexual power of the female leads, reasserting glamour as a mysterious and highly-charged energy.

At this point in time the American film industry was in considerable decline, as television took audiences away from the cinema in its home and overseas markets. The studios were still controlled by the pre-war greats, and new ideas for productions were not realized until the revolution that began with the independent blockbuster, *Easy Rider*, in 1969.

Resisting Hollywood : Post-War Official British Culture

The perceived threat of Hollywood still informed the construction of official British culture and the development of the British film industry throughout the late 1940s and 1950s. Harold Wilson, in his role as President of the Board of Trade, undertook to bolster the British film industry and curtail the influence of Hollywood. The new Labour government was facing a severe economic crisis in 1946, due to foreign exchange problems and debts to America caused by the war. The government had already imposed a tax on the exhibition receipts from American films in August 1947, allowing only 25 per cent of the total out of the country (Swann, 1987: 89). In response, the Motion Picture Association of America decided to cease the export of films to Britain until the tax was lifted. Harold Wilson appeared intransigent in January

1948, announcing to the House of Commons: 'I am sure I can say to Hollywood that if they believe they can squeeze us into modifying our attitude on the duty by continuing the embargo, they are backing a loser' (Swann 1987: 101). However, the Anglo-American Film Agreement, which took effect from June 1948, did exactly that. Hollywood could distribute 180 films in Britain and £17,000,000 out of the country, ith the proviso that the remainder would be reinvested in Britain, largely in the British film industry. Hollywood were also permitted to take more of their earnings out of Britain as a sum equivalent to the earnings of British films in America. This was a comparatively small amount, as British films were only really successful on the 'arthouse' circuit. Hollywood was not overjoyed with the *entente,* particularly the limit on the amount of cash it could take out of Britain, its most lucrative foreign market. The British establishment bemoaned the lack of evidence for a sustainable British film industry. The short-lived British women's magazine *Film and Fashion* berated the Government in April 1948, soon after the agreement had been reached: 'Despite all the assurances of Harold Wilson and our movie magnates we are now facing a more serious menace than ever before . . . Events over the last two months clearly indicate that the British film industry will, to a large extent become Americanised, unless we change our tactics' (p. 5). The Editor urged the British film industry to look to Britain's rich heritage and history, its culture and tradition, for material. The success of Laurence Olivier's *Hamlet* (1948) was regarded as a key example. The magazine also instigated a 'Search for Talent' to find potential British film stars with glamour and potential acting ability.

The efforts of the British government and the British middle-brow press had little effect on the British cinema public, which remained predominantly working-class, as it had been before the war (Swann 1987: 4). Official British efforts to stem the popularity of Hollywood and support the British film industry flopped (Jarvie 1992). Going to the cinema to see Hollywood films remained the most popular pastime in late 1940s and early 1950s Britain. The year 1946 saw the peak of cinema attendance in Britain, with admission receipts totalling £121,000,000. By 1949 this had declined only slightly to 24,000,000 admissions in total. One survey conducted in 1949 found that 40 per cent of adults attended the cinema regularly on a weekly basis (Swann 1987: 36). Apart from the continued economic, cultural and political reasons to limit the import and display of Hollywood films, there was also the moral dimension. There was a further American presence beyond Hollywood film following America's entry into the war. GIs were stationed in the south of England: by June 1944 one and three-quarter million Americans were stationed in and around Hampshire, East Anglia, Cambridgeshire, Burtonwood near Liverpool and London. The GIs brought the American way of life with them, as one teenager in Cambridge recalled: 'To go on one of their bases was absolutely fantastic because there was no shortage of anything. Each base was a little America, with plenty of food and drink and fantastic great iced cakes. Every night you could, you were out. All the girls were doing it. It was a lovely atmosphere. At the dances they were really friendly. They'd just come up and say: "Cut a rug"' (Dimbleby and Reynolds 1988: 151). Some 70,000 British women eventually married American GIs and moved permanently to America. As Joanne Lacey has argued about the presence of GIs near Liverpool: 'They were the physical manifestation of the American Dream on Liverpool's streets. Described in the interviews as "the prizes", the GIs came to function as a cipher for the women's fantasies and aspirations about "America" as the land of plenty and opportunity' (1999: 59). 'Over sexed, over-paid and over here' the presence of the GIs continued to be a source of anxiety for British men and the British élite well into the 1950s (Hebdige 1981a: 43). The British establishment feared the effects of American popular culture on the young, banning the import of American comic books in 1954 (M. Barker 1984). The rash of films made for the youth market also worried the British authorities. There was such moral panic about the behaviour of juvenile delinquents that the film, *The Wild One* (1953), starring Marlon Brando, was banned from public exhibition in Britain for fifteen years.[3] Based as it was on a real-life event when a gang of motorcyclists invaded the small town of Hollister on 4 July 1947, it made the British authorities fear copy-cat invasions in Britain.

The most powerful film to effect the dress and behaviour of British teenagers was *Rock Around the Clock*. Released in Britain in September 1956, it starred Rock and Roller Bill Haley and the Comets, who enjoyed greater popularity in Britain than the US (Harper and Porter 1999: 75). The film inspired riotous behaviour in the cinemas, including jiving in the aisles and trashing the interiors. As the *New York Times* reported: 'Britons are puzzled by the riotous behaviour of the teen-agers who have been moved by rock 'n' roll music to sing and dance wildly in the streets, to slug inoffensive Bobbies and in general to behave in a most un-British fashion' (as quoted by Jahn 1973: 42). One fan recalled:

When the film *Rock Around the Clock* came, everybody went. It seemed our whole generation stood in the cinema aisles, bawling back at the screen the choruses of those songs: 'Razzle dazzle' shouted Bill Hayley, the star of the film. 'Razzle dazzle' we all hollered back. . . . 'See ya later alligator' – that was the days before soccer had hooligans. There was no chanting; on the football terraces it was 'Up the cobblers,' and 'Well done Stanley Matthews.' It was at the cinema we bawled our heads off, 'Shake, rattle and roll' was just what we needed. As if possessed by the devil, and the fit Teds did handstands in the aisles (as quoted in Harper and Porter 1999: 75).

The response of the authorities, including the cities of Birmingham, Liverpool, Bristol and Belfast, was to ban this dangerous film. Teenagers were arrested and punished for their anti-social behaviour. Anthony Bicat described the pandemonium the film caused thus: 'In Manchester, after showing *Rock Around the Clock*, ten youths were fined for insulting behaviour when they left the cinema. Rhythm-crazed youngsters, after they had seen the film, held up traffic for half an hour and trampled in the flower beds in the municipal garden. In Blackburn the Watch Committee banned the film . . . In Croydon the police cleared the David Theatre on Sunday of jiving youngsters' (1970: 324–5). Town councils, the churches, government, academics, the BBC and the British music press were united in their fear of the corrupting influence of rock and roll. Partly based on racism and partly on the fear of social unrest, the strength of the reaction also relates back to British reactions to Hollywood films in the 1920s. The fear of the Americanization of British culture reached back over thirty years: rock and roll was only the latest manifestation, and Hollywood film always its emissary. Elvis Presley was also regarded as a dangerous threat to British youth's morals, and the showing of *Jailhouse Rock* caused further outrage. Elvis's wearing of blue denim jeans in the film further reinforced the currency of that garment amongst teenagers.

Surprisingly, criticism of the new rock and roll lifestyle also came from left- wing academics. One of the founders of cultural studies, Richard Hoggart, wrote of the scene in a coffee bar in his first book, *The Uses of Literacy*, in 1958: 'Compared even with the pub around the corner, this is all a peculiarly thin and pallid form of dissipation, a sort of spiritual dry-rot amid the odour of boiled milk. Many of the customers – their clothes, their hair-styles, their facial expressions all indicate – are living to a large extent in a myth-world compounded of a few simple elements which they take to be those of American life.'

Hoggart looked back nostalgically on the sense of community in his own working-class, pre-war childhood, and resented the American invasion of British cultural values.

Culture Is Good For You

Efforts were made by the British elite to patrol the Council of Industrial Design in 1945, the Arts Council in 1946 and the Institute of Contemporary Arts in the same year. Competition for Hollywood also came from television, although it was less advanced than in the US, with the BBC offering worthy, middle-brow entertainment from the early 1950s and commercial television offering something more popular from 1955. Rationing continued until 1953, and was even more severe than during the war in many cases. Furniture was still rationed under the Utility scheme, launched in 1941. Its styling was restricted to a heavy, English Arts and Crafts look blended with Swedish modernism. Purchased by means of coupons, the pieces were chosen from a catalogue and ordered, most usually through the local co-op. The design establishment were able to dictate the style of what the consumers bought for their homes. This was a dream come true for furniture designer and manufacturer, Gordon Russell, who headed the specialist design panel of the Utility scheme. He welcomed the opportunity to dictate mass taste. He recalled in 1946: 'I felt that to raise the whole standard of furniture for the mass of the people was not a bad wartime job' (McCarthy, 1979: 69). In consequence, wartime consumers were condemned to a restricted choice of bland, Swedish-inspired modernism in furniture. The same was true of fashion, with the Incorporated Society of London Fashion Designers designing practical, well-tailored clothing for the Utility scheme from 1941. Fashion was also restricted in terms of what could be bought ready-made and also of the fabrics available to make up garments. Women during the war and just after had to 'make do and mend', recycling old clothes, restyling hats and using black-out curtains for making evening dresses. Women's magazines were filled with ideas for making the most of what was available. The same sort of advice was offered to women about interior décor during the time of rationing.

The Utility scheme was phased out soon after the war, by which time it had earned a reputation for solid construction but boring designs. As the Mass Observation survey of the *Britain Can Make It* exhibition of British good design revealed: 'The dominant trend is away from Utility. People are searching for something delicate and colourful, which will not remind them of wartime' (Mass Observation Survey 1946).

The exhibition was held at the Victoria and Albert Museum, and was organized by the new Council of Industrial Design, a government body established in 1945 to raise standards in British design in order that the export market, much depleted with the demise of the British Empire, could be boosted with sales to America. George V1 declared in his opening speech at the exhibition in September 1946: 'The Council of Industrial Design is an expression of our national will to improve our commercial prospects and our personal standards of living. . . . Government and industry have worked together to show our own people, and our friends from abroad the newest and the best of our production' (*The Times*, 25 September 1946: 2). *Britain Can Make It* – the title was based on the wartime propaganda film, *Britain Can Take It* – consisted entirely of British design, including electrical appliances, ideal room settings, a fashion display, packaging and an area devoted to the role and working methods of the designer. The exhibition was immensely popular, attracting a total of 1,432,546 visitors. The visitors admired the more colourful displays, but complained about the dullness of Utility and about the fact that most items were labelled 'For Export Only'.

This opinion and overriding trend was largely ignored by the Council of Industrial Design, renamed the Design Council in 1960. The Council persevered in the promotion of European modernism in post-war Britain in opposition to the demands of popular taste. The Council launched the Contemporary Style in 1949 in its magazine for industry and the consumer, *Design*. Like Utility, the Contemporary blended Swedish modern with British traditional design. The style was first seen at the *Festival of Britain*. Held to commemorate the 1851 Crystal Palace exhibition, this celebration of national culture, past and present, was held on the south bank of the Thames in London. The erection of so many new structures on what was a derelict bombsite, although only the Royal Festival Hall was permanent, symbolized a new Britain emerging from the ashes of the war. Struggling to assert a new national identity on a post-colonial world stage, the Festival authorities exploited past traditions combined with a futuristic vision, largely borrowed from the New York World's Fair of 1939. As part of the new Welfare State, which Britain's first majority Labour government established during their term of office from 1945 to 1951, culture was officially supported for the public good. In tandem with the new National Health Service, free education and adequate housing, Welfare State design played an integral part in the Festival. The COID mounted an exhibition of room-settings in the *Home and Garden* pavilion and launched the Design Index, enabling visitors to browse through examples of carefully vetted 'good design' on a card index containing 20,000 black and white photographs. The interiors and furniture designed for the Festival were all judged acceptable by the Council before being put on display. The COID opened its Design Centre in Haymarket, London in 1956. Here the Council continued to campaign for 'good design' under the aegis of the British government, with exhibitions, publications, the Design Index and the annual award to the best of British design. Called 'Design of the Year' when it was founded in 1957, the first awards were given to the Contemporary Style Hille convertible bed-settee designed by Robin Day and David Mellor, *Pride* cutlery, and flatware, designed for Walter and Hall.

Other aspects of official British culture to be promoted nationally included fine art, with the newly founded Arts Council of Great Britain. This propaganda on behalf of modern art grew out of the wartime efforts of the Council for the Encouragement of Music and the Arts, which organized touring exhibitions of modern paintings and musical recitals in factory canteens. Defenders of modernism and high culture were heartened by the results. Tom Harrison, Director of Mass Observation, addressed the Design and Industries Association in 1943. The results were published in *Art and Industry* in September that year, when Harrison reported: 'Take, as Mass Observation has done, a series of pictures by a wide range of artists, and show them to a wide range of ordinary people in an ordinary northern town. The pictures that evoke the strongest and most excited reaction was one by Picasso, and in general all the modern, imaginative, non-photographic painters aroused the greatest interest, often hostile, but often delighted and nearly always positive' (p. 83) Harrison argued that this was because, through the efforts of: 'Sir Kenneth Clark and CEMA the lower section of the public have for the first time been given a rather increased opportunity to see better art'. Hence, throughout the 1950s and 1960s the Arts Council in Britain and the British Council abroad promoted the joys of modern painting and sculpture to the fortunate public. The careers of British artists like Henry Moore were boosted with the direction of official resources to fund modern art in the service of promoting national identity.

New Looks: Glamour, Design and Cinema

The worthy displays of good design offered by the Council of Industrial Design and of fine art by the Arts Council of Great Britain could not compete for popular attention with the growing stream of American imported goods during the 1950s. The attractiveness of the goods was reinforced by the glamour of Hollywood film and American television during the period. The lifestyle depicted on the Hollywood screen and, from 1955, on the small screen in the form of television portrayed America as the land of opportunity and plenty, where everybody had a smart kitchen with a washing machine and open-plan living/dining rooms. Where everyone drove a smart car to their suburban home and ate from well-stocked fridges.

Few families could afford the full American lifestyle; they could only marvel at what was shown on screen. J. P. Mayer's survey of the British cinema audience carried out in the late 1940s elicited a range of illuminating responses to the question of Hollywood and consumer culture, as Paul Swann explains:

> many of Mayer's correspondents, predominately women, noted how they lusted after the clothing and consumer durables they saw in American films. One wrote that she would love to wear clothes like Lana Turner's and have an American-style white kitchen, if the Chancellor of the Exchequer would only let her' (1987: 43).

Those who worked on the ocean liners were amongst the first to bring back from America the new consumer goods just after the war. As Margaret Florence Green, whose stepfather was Chief Quarter Master on the *Queen Mary*, remembered:

> . . .we were very lucky, we were one of the first in our street to have a washing machine and a refrigerator and sweets and food and china. Everything, particularly in those days Woolworth's in America was a big store for the seamen so they used to get taxis from the dockside, because its wasn't safe to walk the New York docks, and they all used to go by taxi to the big stores in America and bring most things home (Massey 1997: 8).

Images of plenty were also exploited in advertising for British goods. The Liverpool firm of Vernons produced kitchen cabinets and boasted 'That Film Kitchen Can Be Yours' inscribed on to a piece of film.

The economic boom effected America sooner than Britain. The expansion in the economy was mainly stimulated by consumer demand. In America the population boomed from 131 million in 1940 to 226 million in 1980. Easy credit was made available during the 1950s, and much of the consumer purchasing during that decade was driven by purchases for the home. New electrical goods became the norm – the purchase of television sets, fridges, washing machines and dishwashers was stimulated and informed by increased advertising. In Britain, when the Prime Minister Harold Macmillan declared in his famous speech of 1957 'You've never had it so good' he reflected popular opinion. With the relaxation of exchange controls in 1958 American goods flowed once more into Britain, just at the time when recovery from wartime and rationing was complete. Increased affluence in Britain was associated with ability to consume an American lifestyle as seen on the cinema screen, on television and in magazines.

What made a dent in cinema attendance figures was the introduction of television, particularly commercial television, in 1955 and the availability of cheaper television sets. The relaxation on hire purchase restrictions in 1954 also triggered demand for TV sets: 3 million licences were issued in 1954, but 8 million in 1958. But Hollywood still reigned supreme in its leadership of glamour, in defining what was desirable in clothing, home decoration and consumer goods throughout the 1950s in Britain.

Anti-American feeling amongst the British elite was further heightened from 1958 onwards when import restrictions were dropped and there was a surge of imports and American investment in Britain. By 1966 there were some 1,600 American subsidiaries or Anglo-American firms in Britain, worth almost $6 billion in terms of investment, America's second largest overseas investment after Canada. The companies employed 6 per cent of the workforce and produced 10 per cent of goods made in British factories. As in the pre-war era, investment was in the manufacture of new consumer goods, such as cars, cosmetics, vacuum cleaners and processed food. Frozen food, TV dinners, supermarkets, barbecues, Tupperware and new, bigger cars were revolutionizing British life. Whilst this led to renewed panic amongst cultural commentators and politicians, for the consumer it meant novelty and fun after the dreary war years.

The lavishness of Christian Dior's New Look in fashion, launched in Paris in 1947, reflected the mood of post-war Britain and the US. Although castigated by the then President of the Board of Trade, Harold Wilson, the look was popular on both sides of the Atlantic and amongst all classes of women. With its padded shoulders, tight waist, full skirts which reached to mid-calf and stiletto heels it was feminine and extravagant. It acted as a counterpoint on behalf of the fashion industry to the rational, functional Utility style with its tailored suits and shirtwaist dresses (Ash and Wilson 1992). The creation of the look in

Paris by a *haute couture* designer and its widespread adoption by the mass market was partly due to cinema. Much like the process whereby art deco was adopted from Paris by Hollywood and consumed in a different form by a mass audience, so the New Look was appropriated by costume designers for the screen. In America the New Look was known as the 'Sweetheart Line', and was first seen on film with Edith Head's creation for Bette Davis in *June Bride* (1948). The full-skirted, feminine dress was used throughout the 1950s to denote femininity, in particular for wedding dresses, as seen in *Father of the Bride* (1950) and *Gentlemen Prefer Blondes* (1953). The starched, formal construction of Dior's New Look, complete with low neckline and corsetry to achieve the nipped-in waistline for the upper-class market, was revised by Hollywood and the mass market, adopting it for more everyday wear in easy-to-care-for fabrics. Seen in action in the 1950s Hollywood musicals such as *Calamity Jane* and *Seven Brides for Seven Brothers* (1954), the skirts whirl around, creating a dizzy display of froth and fabric. As Joanne Lacey's research into the consumption of popular film in Liverpool revealed when recalling Hollywood musicals of the 1950s: 'My interviewees did understand the importance of glamour. Glamour is positioned overwhelmingly as the antithesis of ordinariness, and ordinary was what these women were trying not to be. What space was there in postwar political and social discourses, or indeed in images of working-class women in British films, and in fashion advice pages for working-class women to be extraordinary?' (1999: 64).

My mother recalled feeling extraordinary in Hollywood-inspired dresses. Going to dances at the Co-operative Society at Consett after the war, when she would enjoy wearing and dancing in the full skirts of the New Look. 'I remember buying a black skirt which had three layers – the bottom one being stiff net so that it swished round when you were dancing. I wore ballerina-type pump shoes and a taffeta blouse with puffed sleeves. I remember enjoying dancing around in that – swishing the skirt round. That idea must have come from the cinema' (In interview with author 1998). She would make many clothes at home using paper patterns, and ensure enough volume in the skirts by using layers of starched net. She danced to a mixture of traditional ballroom music, country dance tunes or jazz played by a small local band. The dance hall was a popular attraction during post-war Britain for young, working-class men and women, as exemplified in the British film *Dance Hall* (1950). It also presented a threat to middle-class cultural values (Kirkham: 1995).

The New Look also reinforced the feminine curves, first contro-versially exploited in, according to the poster, 'Howard Hughes' Daring Production – Action! Thrills!! Sensations!!! Primitive Love!!!!' *The Outlaw* (1941). The look continued to be popular during the 1950s, as exempli-fied by popular Hollywood stars, particularly Marilyn Monroe in *Gentlemen Prefer Blondes* (1953), *The Seven Year Itch* (1955) and *Bus Stop* (1956). It was lamely imitated by Jayne Mansfield in *The Girl Can't Help It* (1956) and *Will Success Spoil Rock Hunter?* (1957). Women in Britain could copy the obvious curves of Hollywood by various means. One was the 'Whirlpool Bra', a solid item of undergarment where the cup was constructed out of a spiral of supportive wire or stitching to give a pronounced profile. In *Vogue*, November 1952, the Berlei Whirlpool Hollywood-Maxwell brassière was advertised as: 'The most glamorous brassiere ever designed. Here's the star of the American fashion scene . . . favourite bra of fashion models, film stars, debutantes – sure to be your favourite too . . . each bust cup a whirlpool of continuous stitching to give firm, flattering uplift, deeply defined separation . . .'. Women could also buy 'Cuties', or latex pads that could be worn inside the bra to give the effect of extra volume and uplifted profile (Figure 43). An advert for the product in *True Stories* of the late 1940s recommended 'Cuties . . . as worn by Stage and Screen Stars. Originated in Hollywood – now available to you. Scientifically designed latex sponge pads, which are porous and can be worn next to the skin in perfect comfort. Cuties fit in your Brassiere and create a natural, modern and youthful **UPLIFT** outline. For wear under swim suits, sweaters, evening gowns and dresses.'

Hollywood star endorsement of beauty products continued unabated during the 1950s. Most prevalent was Max Factor, the Hollywood cosmetics manufacturer, who by 1950 was selling make-up on a global scale to women in countries as diverse as Australia, South Africa, Ireland, Brazil, Italy, Japan and India, plus nearly 100 more. Advertisements were placed in the burgeoning number of women's and film fan magazines and in the *Ideal Home Yearbook*. Just after the war came the 'Colour Harmony Make-Up of the Stars' range, with adverts featuring Esther Wild, Deborah Kerr, Betty Hutton and Rhonda Fleming. Face powder, lipstick, eye shadow and 'pancake' foundation were sold as: 'These famous glamorizing requisites of Hollywood's most alluring screen stars will give you amazing new beauty RIGHT NOW! Try them today . . . this very night' (*Woman's Own*, 15 December 1949: 17) (Figure 44). The emphasis on colour in the range and the use of luridly coloured press advertising reflected Hollywood's new Technicolor orientation.

Figure 43 Advertisement for Cuties Breast Enhancers

In 1949 'Pan-Stik' was developed by Max Factor Junior as a non-greasy foundation contained in a tube that could be pushed up by turning the base and applied straight to the skin. Margaret Florence Green, who worked on the Docks Telephone Exchange at Southampton during the 1950s, recalled of the period: 'Deborah Kerr, Rita Hayworth, of course, because cinema was our only entertainment in those days, to go on the dockside and to see them arrive on the *Queen Mary* and particularly the fashions and the make-up, which was Max Factor, everybody had to buy a Max Factor Pan-Stik because that was the thing that everybody used. Make-up was very heavy, not very natural in those days and the clothes were very glamorous, very glamorous' (Massey: 1997: 9) (Figure 45).

Other brands of make-up also used the kudos of Hollywood to sell their products. Tangee 'New, True Red-Red!' was sold by association with Hollywood starlet Marsha Hunt, and Tokalon lipstick was advertised

heavy pouts and concrete curls of the beauties of the period were a million miles away from anything I could ever hope or want to look like; the hour-glass fashions simply didn't suit me. Of course I would never look like Audrey Hepburn either, but at least she demonstrated that there was, after all, another way to be (Cook and Dodd 1993: 36).

Similarly, Barbara Hulanicki, the founder of the leading young fashion store of the late 1960s, *Biba*, remembered: 'Sabrina Fair made a huge impact on us all . . . everyone walked around in black, sloppy sweaters, suede low-cut flatties and gold hoop earrings . . . Audrey Hepburn and Givenchy were made for each other. His little black dress with shoestring straps in Sabrina Fair must have been imprinted on many teenagers' minds forever' (Cook and Dodd 1993: 37). My mother had her hair specially cut just like hers in Newcastle after seeing *Roman Holiday* (1953). As a student of art at teacher training college, the Americanized left-bank glamour of Hepburn suited her values and aspirations at the time. Hepburn's collaboration with Hollywood and the Parisian couturier, Givenchy, is typical of America's colonization of 'high culture' after the war, just as Hollywood's costume designers appropriated the Parisian New Look and recreated it in patchwork for *Seven Brides for Seven Brothers*.

Teenager Fashion

It was the young adult age group who benefited the most from the increased affluence of the post-war era. Before the 1950s people between the ages of sixteen and twenty-five had simply mirrored their parents in mode of dress and taste in music. However, this changed when teenagers became a recognizably different category of potential customers with a separate identity to that of their parents. The term or concept of the teenager was an American creation. As Mark Abrams, the market researcher, observed in his important survey, commissioned by the London Press Exchange in 1959, on *The Teenage Consumer*: 'Postwar Britain has little experience in providing for prosperous working class teenagers; the latter have therefore, in shaping their consumption standards and habits, depended very heavily on the one industrial country that has such experience, the United States' (1959 : 19). The survey also revealed the spending power of the teenager in the previous year to be £900 million. The teenagers were in employment or at college, with few financial responsibilities. They were able to express their own identity through the consumer goods they bought and the clothes they wore. Whilst British cultural commentators feared that youths were being brainwashed by American popular music and films, they were expressing a new form of identity. Despite these measures the code of dress established by film was highly influential, disseminated by magazines, private screenings of films at, for example, the ICA, and record covers. Marlon Brando had already appeared in slob T-shirt in *A Streetcar Named Desire* in 1951. Then regarded as an item of men's underwear or workman's clothing, the tight-fitting T-shirt offended the sensitive Blanche, but showed Brando's mean muscles. Brando is rumoured to have provided his own clothing for *The Wild One*, which consisted of white T-shirt again, airforce flying jacket and boots with jeans (Bruzzi 1997: 7). This contrasts starkly with the flouncy New Look of the small-town girls attracted to the gang in the film. The narrative was based on the Hollister Bash of 4 July 1947. Here the American Motorcycle Association (AMA) had arranged races in the sleepy Californian town of Hollister. Over 4,000 motorcyclists turned up for the event, which was then inflated out of all recognition in *Life* magazine of 21 July 1947, with posed photographs and hysterical text. This was one of the first mass media examples of the labelling of motorcyclists as the 'other', as a threat to the norms of respectable society. The feeling of alienation from the values and aspirations of the next generation was portrayed in *Rebel Without a Cause* (1955), starring James Dean as Jim in irreverent white T-shirt, red windbreaker, jeans and brylcreemed quiff. It wasn't only Dean's clothes that caused a stir, but his attitude, and the way this attitude was portrayed on the screen, with hunched shoulders and swaggering walk. Blue jeans became so popular in late 1950s America that the American Institute of Men's and Boys' Wear mounted a campaign in American high schools to attempt to stem the popularity of denim-wearing, to little effect (Constantino: 1997).

Hollywood and Modernism

With the onset of the Cold War and the construction of America as the leader of the Free World, the appropriate representation of this leadership was played out in cultural terms. Before the war America had undoubtedly enjoyed command of the best of popular culture. With the advent of the Cold War America also consciously occupied the cultural high ground as well. This was aided by America's superior command of the mass media, which included Hollywood film. For example, Jackson Pollock was immortalized on the pages of *Life* magazine in 1952, as American artists could serve to establish a distinctive bohemian glamour while yet still fulfilling the propaganda purposes of the United States government. Abstract Expressionism was consciously marketed in Europe as the latest avant-garde movement, and tremendous efforts were made to replace Paris with New York as the centre of the Western art world (Guilbaut 1984; Massey 1995). Likewise, modern architecture and design were reworked to represent the values of a successful liberal regime rather than their earlier left-wing associations. While the British Council of Industrial Design's worthy efforts to promote the solid benefits of British good design continued, a far more attractive American version reached British cinema audiences and made far more impact. Moreover, when commercial television began transmission in 1955, imported shows like *I Love Lucy*, first shown on ITV in 1956, were a successful showcase for modern American interior design and consumer products. The avant-garde architects who had fled persecution in pre-war Germany now enjoyed flourishing careers on the east coast of America. The former Bauhaus student and furniture teacher, Marcel Breuer, designed a single-storey modern version of a ranch house at Huntington, Long Island. Reviewing this building, featured in the British *Ideal Home Book* of 1956 as an example of 'Lessons of the American Home', J. C. Palmes regretted the propensity for 'the British house . . . being built to the same old stereotyped plan – under the assumption that every household was forever ordained to have servants to lay the fires, answer the front and back doors, carry the brass water cans upstairs, wait at table and be banished at most other times to the back premises' (p. 12). However, it was the architecture and design developed on the West Coast of America that made the most impact on nearby Hollywood and on British designers and design theorists.

The British architect and member of the Independent Group, Alison Smithson, celebrated the work of West Coast designers Charles and Ray Eames in a special issue of *Architectural Design* in September 1966. For Smithson: 'The Eames support the West coast world for us and help support our European dream of America as a great free place to be in' (Smithson and Smithson 1966: 448). She describes trying to source a modern chair in the early 1950s in Britain: 'It was the world of the horrors of the Festival of Britain and so on. The Eames chair was like a message of hope from another planet.' For young, modernist designers of the 1950s in Britain the Eameses and their West Coast stylishness were an inspiring influence in the days of worthy Welfare State culture sanctioned by the Council of Industrial Design. Moreover, Smithson uses reference to the contemporary film genres of horror and science fiction to frame her argument.

The more organic, West Coast school of modernism had its roots in the Cranbrook Academy of Art during the 1930s–1950s, where Charles and Ray Eames first met. Charles Eames was teaching by this point, and won the Organic Design competition at the Museum of Modern Art in 1940 with Eero Saarinen. Charles and Ray married in 1941, and established their practice in the then derelict area of Venice in Los Angeles. Between 1945 and 1978 more than 40 furniture designs went into production, while the couple were also responsible for making more than 80 films (Kirkham 1995). The Eameses represented the Hollywood ideal in terms of design practice. Working at times for Billy Wilder, designing a couch for his office, for example, they did mingle with the Hollywood set. Their own home also promoted West Coast modernism (Figure 46). Built in Pacific Palisades in 1945, it was part of the Case Study series initiated by the Editor of *Arts and Architecture* magazine, John Entenza, built in picturesque Los Angeles settings to demonstrate the West Coast's modern design abilities. Another reason for the Case Study series was to demonstrate the possibilities of building homes from prefabricated, standardized parts at a time of shortages of housing for troops returning from the war.

Another member of the Independent Group, Lawrence Alloway, visited America in 1958 on a State Department grant. Visiting every major city in the US, he arrived in Los Angeles on 1 June to be shepherded around by fellow critic Jules Langsmer. Writing to Sylvia Sleigh on the second day after his arrival he enthused: 'We went to the Eames last night until 2.00 in the morning. They just got back. I've been in 2 different swimming pools already: great. Got wonderful summer clothes at Onbachs (you know – the cat ad in Time). I have equipped myself for hot sunny LA for about $10 – pants, shirts, the lot. Wonderful feeling to be in Hollywood at last – only seen one movie actor but I feel so at home and so would you. Hospitable feeling, trees, low houses, swimming pools, drinks, lemon trees around the pool. I am absolutely sold on LA.' Alloway was eventually to move to New York in 1961, realizing that the social barriers that existed in the London art world precluded him from ever succeeding there. In New York he was accepted more for what he was, an intellectual and knowledgeable cultural critic, for the skills he had to offer. By the early 1960s New York's leadership of the global avant-garde was secured with the successes of Abstract Expressionism and the burgeoning reputation of American Pop Art. American modernism had come to represent liberal,

Figure 46 Charles and Ray Eames at Home in Hollywood

democratic values, represented by fresh technicolor movies, huge abstract canvasses and a vast consumer culture. Charles and Ray Eames celebrated this in Moscow in 1959 when they presented a multi-media exhibition on behalf of the United States government that featured the growing suburbia of America. Eames furniture was recommended by *Playboy* magazine in October 1956 as part of 'Playboy's Penthouse Apartment', where: 'a man, perhaps like you, can live in masculine elegance . . . a fine place to live and love and be merry, a place to relax in alone or to share for intimate hours with some lucky lass' (p. 65).

Pierre Koenig, like the Eameses, designed a steel-framed house for the 'Case Study' series in the late 1950s. With flat roof, open spaces and Eames modern furniture, it represented the new, all-powerful democracy in action. Koenig served in the American army during the war, and was amongst the group that discovered Auschwitz. He recovered from the shock by using his belief in the redeeming values of modernism: 'By that time, we were so up to our eyes in horror that it was a case, when we got home, of either giving in and saying that there was no such thing as a future, that the Nazis had destroyed forever the notion of human progress, or of just the opposite: fighting for a Modern world in which progress was all' (*The Guardian Weekend*: 7 November 1998: 82). The publicity shots for Koenig's houses in the 1950s were straight out of Hollywood, with the architect in well-cut suit and Tony Curtis haircut and the model in New Look blue chiffon, bright red lipstick and auburn hair.

All Hollywood films used the latest in interior design the backdrop for their domestic comedies, from the romantic comedies and women's films to science fiction. Alloway, commenting on the MGM science-fiction classic, *Forbidden Planet* (1956), described it as: 'West Coast Architecture extrapolated as a setting for leisure on the planet Altair 4' (1958: 85).

The Independent Group were not, by and large, conventionally educated public school and Oxbridge graduates, and this explains the members' ready acceptance of Hollywood cinema as a legitimate object of academic study, source of design inspiration and object of critical discourse. They had been to art school or had not been to school at all, as in the case of Lawrence Alloway, who suffered childhood tuberculosis and was taught at home by his mother. They rightly perceived this to be a barrier to success in the London art scene: for example, according to his widow, Alloway tried to obtain writing work on the *New Statesman*, but after he had been asked what school he went to, the work was refused. They also genuinely admired mass culture, and operated as knowing consumers. As Alloway recalled in 1977:

One of the things about all of us in the Independent Group was that we had little education, we all of us were non-University people and therefore popular culture was something we'd grown up with and it hadn't been interrupted. If you go to university or college your natural possession of the mass media is interrupted by all the other demands upon your time. Ours hadn't been, so we just naturally went on looking at the films and the ads and magazines that we grew up with. So the sociology was not an objective, external study, it was part of ourselves (Interview conducted for *Fathers of Pop* p. 8).

Alloway contributed to the development of serious analysis of Hollywood cinema in Britain through his contributions to and support of *Movie* magazine and *ARK*, the magazine of the Royal College of Art, plus his talks and organization of activities at the ICA. He was the first critic to use his genuine enthusiasm for cinema to inform his writing. He described the thrill of going to the Empire cinema in London's Leicester Square in a piece on 'Architecture and the Modern Cinema' for *The Listener*, recalling: 'Entering it, whether to see Greta Garbo's first talkie, *Gone with the Wind* on its first run, or *Ben Hur*, was really living. You passed under a grandiose coffered gilt ceiling; down or up wide, gently curved stairs; through halls lined with wall-size engraved mirrors doubling up the candelabra; like sets for *The Phantom of the Opera*' (June 22 1961: 1085). Ian Cameron paid homage in 1990 to his 'widely quoted article' for *Movie* in February/March 1963. 'The Iconography of the Movies' urged traditional film critics to move beyond the French *auteur* approach and consider popular film in broader terms. Again he stressed the personal experience of being a genuine film fan. 'The meaning of a single movie is inseparable from the larger pattern of content-analysis of other movies. And the point is, that his knowledge, of concepts and themes, is the common property of the regular audience of the movies' (p. 8). Alloway also astutely wrote about the impact of widescreen projection in 'The Arts and the Mass Media' in *Architectural Design* in 1958. 'In reaction to the small TV screen, movie makers spread sideways (CinemaScope) and back into space (Vista-Vision). All the regular film critics opposed the new array of shapes, but all have been accepted by the audiences' (February 1958, pp. 84–5). Indeed, it was the effects of colour and the widescreen that characterized going to the pictures in 1950s Britain.

Swinging London: Hollywood and Pop

The change from Cold War modernism to the glamour of youth and anti-establishment challenges came as part of a British pop revolution in film and design. 'The Challenge of Pop' was the title of a famous article that Paul Reilly wrote for *Architectural Review* in 1967. Reilly was Director of the COID at the time, and acknowledged that the old style values of the classic modern movement had been usurped by a new, young, pop aesthetic. 'Carnaby Street and King's Road, Chelsea, with their meagre buildings, ephemeral graphics and idiosyncratic fashions, are the world-wide symbols of a new, emancipated, classless generation' (p. 256). America looked to Britain for leadership in terms of youth culture. *Time* magazine featured 'London – The Swinging City' as its main feature and cover story in April 1966. This revolution in taste and style was partly played out through film. The Beatles had three number one hits in Britain in 1963, and toured America in the following year. They had originally dressed in the conventional attire of the rocker, with black leather bike jackets and T-shirts. However, their new manager, Brian Epstein, smartened the band up in 1962. Made by show business tailor Dougie Millings, the Beatle suits were based on designs by Pierre Cardin. The jackets had no collars and were extremely short, with no vents at the back. The distinctiveness of The Beatles' visual style was further played out by the cover of their third LP, *A Hard Day's Night*, released in 1964, which carried four black-and-white photographs of each Beatle carrying different expressions. The Beatles music was excellent, and the combination of this with the action of the documentary-style film, *A Hard Day's Night,* directed by Dick Lester, was tremendously exciting and completely novel. The band progressed in 1967 to produce their album, *Sergeant Pepper's Lonely Heart's Club Band*, with a montage cover designed by the British pop artist Peter Blake. Included were images of male and female Hollywood stars, including Marilyn Monroe and Marlon Brando (from *Rebel Without a Cause*), surrounding the Beatles dressed in satin pastiches of Victorian military uniforms. Just as Hollywood had provided a useful metaphor for the Independent Group's attack on stuffy British attitudes to popular design, so images from classical Hollywood cinema were reworked from the late 1960s as provocative emblems of a lost age of glamour. The images flew in the face of British respectability and modernism. Hollywood was still regarded as feminine, frivolous and vulgar during the 1960s amongst a generation of designers, architects and cultural critics who had grown up during the 1930s. However, for those who had reached adulthood during the 1950s and 1960s classical Hollywood was a remote dream that could be revisited as a possible site of pleasure and decadence, and so could challenge the hegemony of masculine modernism. Hollywood imagery was used in Britain during the late 1960s in the same manner as contemporary advertising imagery or

Victorian popular culture to challenge the existing canons of respectable modernism.

The American film industry was to resurrect itself around independent cinema during the late 1960s, when the death of classical Hollywood was finally acknowledged. The West Coast modernism seen in *Forbidden Planet* was superseded by the acid colours and amoeboid shapes of pop. Stanley Kubrick's *2001: A Space Odyssey* (1968) featured futuristic furniture by the French designer Olivier Mourgue. Science fiction sets were decorated with low seating constructed from steel tube with foam lining, covered in brilliantly coloured nylon jersey. The challenge of pop from Britain, relayed partly by means of popular film, fed into the creation of a post-modern sensibility.

Notes

1. Small local cinemas were often badly maintained and not at all glamorous. As one interviewee, Mrs Manner-Travers, recalled in the York Oral History Project (1988): 'Oh, it was cosy. It was all in that colour gold velvet. Plush curtains full of fleas. I used to go home with fleas on me. And the seats were gold plush. And when the matinée first started we used to go round with all this spraying. Oh it used to smell lovely' (pp. 54–5). Mrs Lloyd Jones also remembered of the Rialto in York: 'the curtains were the most dramatic part, 'cause these were black velvet and had those red and green stripes across the bottom. Huge patterns which were very dramatic. But it was the ABC which had the swagged curtains, which were really the epitome, weren't they? Art deco. But I do remember, I think it was after the '47 flood there was always – ever after that – about two feet up the curtain there was this nasty water mark which they never managed to get out. I remember that for quite some time after that you would only go in the balcony, because they had quite a problem with rats' (p. 44).

2. The Rank Charm School was established in 1946 by Rank to emulate the Hollywood studio system of establishing and promoting stars. The Rank Publicity Department organized and distributed signed photographs of the starlets, who travelled the country attending beauty contests and film premières. The venture was doomed, mainly because the ersatz Hollywood stars all looked the same and lacked the same vehicles for stardom on offer to their American counterparts.

3. The film *The Wild One* was shown at private cinemas in Britain, including the ICA, at the time of its release.

Post-Modern Glamour:
A Postscript

By 1967 the pop revolution in design, art and film had passed, along with Britain's brief leadership of glamour. The Beatles appeared on the cover of *Sergeant Pepper's Lonely Hearts Club Band* in June 1967 with unkempt hair reaching their shoulders and Victorian military uniforms made from acid-coloured satins. This form of post-modern styling reworked past looks in an ironic and self-conscious manner as an effective challenge to mainstream modernism. Hollywood glamour was revived as part of this challenge and worn by both men and women – it remained a feminine attribute, and was exploited by men in a deliberate attempt to appear effeminate. The centre of leadership for this dangerous and edgy glamour was the west coast of America, not Los Angeles as in the 1930s, but San Francisco. The 1930s Hollywood glamour was revived by film-makers, fashion designers and interior decorators to represent the spirit of hedonistic disdain for all the established values of the previous generation. Popular culture also became marginally more acceptable for academics to study and partake in. Hollywood and Las Vegas became symbols for relativism in architectural writing about post-modernism.

Post-Classical Hollywood

The revival of Hollywood came from a new crop of young, experimental film-makers emerging from the film courses at UCLA. The founding generation of studio contract directors had all left film-making by 1970. John Ford, Howard Hawks, Frank Capra, Douglas Sirk, George Stevens, King Vidor and Raoul Walsh had all left the creative arena (Sklar 1994: 322). *Bonny and Clyde* was a risky project pioneered by Hollywood outsider, the actor Warren Beatty. The film had an inauspicious launch

Figure 47 Still from *Easy Rider*

in America in September 1967, but enjoyed a positive reception in London, with Faye Dunaway's beret adopted immediately as fashionable wear (Biskind 1998: 45). The film reworked the 1930s gangster theme and revived interest in 1930s fashion for both men and women. The costumes were designed by Theadora van Runkle, who was nominated for an academy award for her designs, for what was her first venture in film. *Bonnie and Clyde*'s heady combination of sex and comparatively graphic violence guaranteed its popularity amongst a young audience and its critical success. It also guaranteed its unpopularity amongst the older generation at Hollywood and everywhere else. The trend was reinforced by another low-budget success, *The Graduate* (1967), which also challenged orthodox values with Dustin Hoffman in his first leading role, seduced by an older married woman.

Most controversial and most influential of all the independently made, low-budget films was *Easy Rider* (1969) (Figure 47). It was genuinely born of the new drug counter-culture – its two creators, Dennis Hopper and Peter Fonda, were central players in the Haight-Ashbury scene from 1966 onwards. Fonda had starred in a motorcycle film, the rather stilted *The Wild Angels* (1966), in which genuine Hell's Angels feature on their customized Harley Davidsons. *Easy Rider* held up a mirror to the new counter-culture in America and presented an avant-garde, low-budget film that featured dope smoking, cocaine snorting and LSD trips to the hippy generation. In tune with the new entrepreneurial spirit of the counter-culture, the film cost only $501,000 to make and grossed $19.1 million in rentals. In Britain it presented an ideal lifestyle to young people who yearned for something beyond the materialism of cosy suburbanism. The lifestyle portrayed, of young, rootless bikers on a quest travelling south through America's badlands was immensely appealing. The fringed buckskin jacket worn by Dennis Hopper was an important feature of counter-culture wear. Inspired by native American prototypes, it was used to great effect on stage at Woodstock by Roger Daltry of *The Who*, and worn by David Crosby of Crosby, Stills, Nash and Young. It also looked great when riding a motorcycle, the fringes blowing in the wind from your outstretched arms. Jackets in this style were available in Britain on a mass-market basis from Lewis Leathers, based in London. It was the motorcycles that made the biggest impact in Britain. The poster of Peter Fonda (Wyatt, after Captain America) and Dennis Hopper (Billy, after Billy the Kid) riding their motorcycles became *de rigueur* in every young hippy's room. Twinned with a powerful underground music soundtrack, the depiction of freewheeling outlaws eventually martyred by 'straight' society was an effective and poignant one.

Hollywood, Hot Rods and Choppers

Customizing, that is altering standard motor vehicles to improve performance and looks, had begun in America in 1920. Modifications were made to the Ford Model T through the availability of custom-made body shells and performance engine parts. The customizing of standard cars escalated in the 1930s, when the hot rod style was created for racing. 'Hot' signified modification, and 'rod' was an abbreviation of 'roadster', as in the Model T roadster. The hot rods were constructed for speed and appearance, with a lowered centre of gravity produced by cutting down the roof pillars (hence the term 'chopped'), souping-up engines, and stripping off all unnecessary decoration or bolt-on parts, so that wings, bonnets and bumpers would be discarded. The impetus for the early hot rod style was street and track racing, with similar trends taking place in motorcycle customizing before the Second World War. During the post-war era in America the customized Harley-Davidson became the mount of the disaffected ex-GI, as epitomized in *The Wild One* (1954). The American doyen of the New Journalism, Tom Wolfe, recounted his visit to the Hot Rod and Custom Car Show in New York in the early 1960s in the introduction to his first book, *The*

Kandy-Kolored Tangerine-Flake Streamline Baby (1968 [1965]). He was working at the time for the New York *Herald Tribune*, and wrote the normal 'totem story' about the show. As he recalled: 'All the totem newspapers would regard one of these shows as a sideshow, a pan-opticon, for creeps and kooks; not even wealthy and eccentric creeps and kooks, which would be all right, but lower class creeps and nutballs with dermatitic skin and ratty hair. The totem story usually makes what is known as "gentle fun" of this, which is a way of saying, don't worry, these people are nothing' (1968: 9). Wolfe then was sponsored by *Esquire* magazine, who published much of his early writing, to visit the centre of the custom scene in California. He interviewed and observed various customizers, most importantly George Barris, owner of Kustom City in North Hollywood. He discovered that the teenage creators of hot rods were challenging the modernist principles of art and design, as epitomized by the Dutch De Stijl artist, Piet Mondrian. They were using the discredited *moderne* style as an alternative to the strictly functional and linear modern. 'The Mondrian principle, those straight edges, is very tight, very Apollonian. The streamline principle, which really has no function, which curves around and swoops and flows just for the thrill of it, is a very free Dionysian' (1968 [1965]: 70).

By 1969 and the release of *Easy Rider* styling had altered to the more radical chopper. Peter Fonda's mount is a customized Harley-Davidson panhead. These engines were produced between 1948 and 1965, this being a 1952–5 model. The front forks have been extended and the neck – where the forks join the frame – raked to accommodate the expanded angle. Customizers had lengthened standard Harley-Davidson forks by a modest two inches before the War to enhance the handling; by 1969 extensions had reached one foot or more. In the case of Fonda's bike the extension is 12 inches over stock, to enable a laid-back riding style where the rider is tilted back with legs outstretched in relaxed cowboy style. The non-standard ape-hanger handlebars enhance the cowboy post still further. Extra chrome has been added, along with a custom banana seat and a small peanut petrol tank, used to accentuate the dimensions of the engine, decorated with special stars and stripes paintwork. The exhaust pipes have been upswept, and rather than a single pipe following the lines of the bottom frame rail, two pipes echo the exaggerated angle of the forks and handlebars. The sissy bar, so-called because it prevents the passenger from sliding backwards off the seat, is extended well beyond the point of practicality. Customized to Fonda's personal specifications, it is an expression of individuality: no longer a practical street performance bike, more a laid back, boulevard cruiser.

Easy Rider made a massive impact on the motorcycle scene in Britain when it was released. As the motorcyclist Odgie recalled: '1969 marked a watershed with the release, in the UK, of the American biker movie, "Easyrider". ... I can still remember seeing them in the film – the first "chopper" motorcycles. Suddenly everyone was buying "apehanger" handlebars, so high you could hardly reach them, and bolting on longer "extended" forks, tiny petrol tanks, minimal seat' (Birmingham Museum and Art Gallery 1994: 11). Before the film it was mainly the café racer style that dominated British customizing, with drop-down handle bars and single racing seat on British bikes like BSAs, Triumphs and Nortons ridden by Rockers. Now the hugely different style of the Harley-Davidson, with extended forms, raked neck, extra chrome and special paintwork, was the new ideal. Stripped of all unnecessary cumbersome luggage or functional exhaust systems, the look was long, lean and mean. In Britain Harleys were in short supply owing to the expense of shipping them over from the States, and so old Triumphs, BSAs and Ariels were customized for the unsuitable British roads in unsuitable British weather. The bike style had been created for comfort on the great sunny American freeways, and it did not translate to the country roads of Britain in the pouring rain. The founding fathers of the British customizing scheme were Leon and Wallace, located in Putney, and Uncle Bunt in East Anglia, who both imported American custom goods by Jammer and Drag Specialities for mail order as well as Harley-Davidsons. Kustom Korner in Crawley, West Sussex, the name of which echoed Kustom City in California, also supplied American parts and paint. This included new types of paint such as metal-flake, where particles of mylar dyed in different colours are suspended in a clear lacquer that can then be sprayed over a base colour. The flakes were diamond- or star-shaped to catch the light effectively.

The initial inspiration of the film *Easy Rider* was reinforced by material beyond the screen with the publication of the magazine, *Easyriders*. Established in 1971 in California, it features choppers created by the magazine's readers. The photographs often include the owner's girl-friend and pet to reinforce the identity of the creator. Links are made between the person and the motorcycle – how the bike was built, what were the local conditions, is he dark and broody or extrovert. There have been claims that such customization should be revered as a craft or popular art, or of the amateur designer, for example, in the exhibition *BikeArt* at Birmingham's Gas Hall held in 1994. This is to reinvent customizing within the acceptable limitations of middle-class notions of good taste, as Peter Stanfield argued in the exhibition catalogue

(1994). Nor should this be understood in a Marxist sense as the revenge of the repressed against the establishment, as resistance through rituals whereby subcultures manipulate oppositional symbols to express their discontent with the world as they find it (Hall *et al.* 1976). Dick Hebdige's cursory treatment of customizing scooters in 'Object as Image: The Italian Scooter Cycle' emphasizes the Mods' use of the scooter as 'Weapons of Exclusion' (1981b) to establish difference from other teenage subcultures and the older generation. It is their deliberate exclusion from the mainstream, mass-produced world of post-war British society that Hebdige celebrates. The theories of Gramsci empower such groups within the hegemonic process: they are marginalized along with all the other 'Others'. A point reinforced by J. T. Borhek in 1989, when he argued: 'Rodding, chopping and restoring are collective attacks on the most distinct characteristic of mass culture; standardized, mass produced consumer goods designed to become obsolete and be discarded' (1989: 97).

Such accounts create a romanticized customizing utopia outside mainstream manufacturing, where the masses revolt against the supposed manipulating forces of marketing and advertising by creating their own fantasy consumer goods. This is a reversion back to the good/bad consumption debate. As Colin Campbell has argued, modern consumption serves the needs of individuals' daydreams, which are not mechanically determined by economics or status. Products are aids to constructing private dreams, the 'material for illusory enjoyment' (1987: 91). This illusory enjoyment comes from the design, construction and use of the customized motorcycle – enacted by Fonda and Hopper. The main point is to create an individualized object by yourself with as little professional help as possible. American firms like Jammer sell the expensive bolt-on parts in mail-order catalogues; but to rake the frame and dispense with the suspension is a skilled job. The individuals, like the heroes of *Easy Rider*, become their machines. Their individuality is expressed through the mechanical means of their transport. I rushed to the cinema to see *Easy Rider* in 1969 at the age of 14, missing a day from school. I have never seen a film up to that point or subsequently that has affected me so deeply. I identified completely with the non-materialistic values of the film, the sense of alienation and thirst for freedom and independence. It reinforced the total hippy lifestyle that I attempted to live out in the north-east of England. I wore a black leather jacket with fringes on the arms. I customized my own motor-cycle with metal-flake paints bought by mail order from Kustom Korner. I loved the feeling of freedom riding on the back of loud, fast motorcycles, particularly as you didn't have to wear a helmet until 1973. I hung out with bikers and Hell's Angels throughout the 1970s, and always owned and rode my own bike until 1982. As a woman on a motorcycle I enjoyed the reaction I created. I fell in love my husband because of the knowledge he displayed about Harley Davidsons whilst we watched *The Wild Angels* on video in a shared house I lived in. Moreover, he actually owned a Harley Davidson, which was rare in Newcastle in 1982. Other films to strike a chord with what I thought of at the time as my rebel soul included *One Flew Over the Cuckoo's Nest*, which re-enacted my own conflicts with authority at school. The film of *Woodstock* also made a big impact when it was impossible to see bands like *The Who* in Newcastle or observe the West Coast, hippy lifestyle firsthand. An important part of the 1970s hippy look was the use of second-hand clothes, their mixing and matching and reinvention as something else. I made a pair of pink satin flared trousers from a New Look evening dress given to me rather too trustingly by my aunt. I made floor-length dresses from bedspreads and lace curtains; I rummaged around at every jumble sale and charity shop for box-shouldered fur coats and crêpe dresses. This interest in antique clothing was also echoed in the reinvention of Victorian period furniture. I painted an ornate Victorian washstand with purple gloss paint, and draped fringed shawls over a 1930s three-piece suite. This 1970s interest in pre-war fashion was also stimulated by *The Great Gatsby* (1974), with Mia Farrow in pastel, diaphanous flapper dresses by Theoni V. Aldredge and Robert Redford's double-breasted, pinstripe suits by Ralph Lauren. As the British comedian and actor, Stephen Fry, recalled of the period: 'At this time at King's Lynn I began to dress, in accordance with the latest vogue, in suits with very baggy trousers, their cut inspired by the Robert Redford version of *The Great Gatsby* which had just been released. I wore stiff detachable collars and silk ties, well-polished shoes and, occasionally, a hat of some description' (Fry 1998: 377–8). *The Sting* had come out in the previous year, and again had recreated the glamour of the 1930s with costumes by Edith Head. This came about as part of a deep-rooted questioning of the values of modernism.

Glamour and Post-Modern Style

An important feature of post-modern questioning of deep-seated values was the revival of 1930s Hollywood glamour. Just as Wolfe observed the customizers' identification with streamlining, so glamour was revived and celebrated in fine art, interior decoration and fashion. Its revival also informed the development of post-modern architectural criticism. Just as the traditional structures and personalities of the world's most powerful film industry had disintegrated and were superseded by a younger, independent clutch of film-makers, so the Hollywood of the past was reconstructed as a self-conscious parody of glamour. For example, the boutique Biba, established as a mail-order company in 1963, recreated the luxury and glamour of pre-war department store shopping and Hollywood film stars (Figure 48). At the time when Andy Warhol produced the Marilyn Monroe and Elvis Presley screenprint series, Barbara Hulanicki created a dark and mysterious environment with fake leopard-skin seats and *moderne* styling. The clothes Biba produced also drew on the dress of 1930s Hollywood stars. Cream silk, bias-cut dresses, feather boas, ankle-strapped shoes, turbans, double-breasted suits for men with matching trilbies, wide ties, two-tone shoes, dark, vamp eye make-up all revived the 1930s look. Biba moved into the Derry and Toms department store building in 1973. This huge shop on Kensington Church Street, complete with roof garden, was originally designed by Bernard George in *moderne* style and had opened in 1933. Since its glamorous heyday it had been neglected, and was acquired by Biba in the romantic hope of reviving its past ambience. A total of £5 million was lavished on the project, which was co-ordinated by the firm of Whitmore-Thomas with help from the John Grasemark Film design studio. There were glamorous Hollywood touches: for example in the Mistress Room fake leopard skin was used to decorate storage boxes, cushions and the *chaise longue*. Other fashion designers also drew on the inspiration of camp Hollywood in Britain, including Ossie Clark, with heavy crêpe, floor-length clinging dresses. Ken Russell, the British film director, in 1971 made *The Boy Friend*, which featured the model Twiggy in 1930s revival Hollywood glamour against the backdrop of Busby Berkeley routines. The revival of classical Hollywood glamour was also evident in popular music of the 1970s, with British bands like Roxy Music and T-Rex manipulating the images of male and female stars. Bryan Ferry the lounge lizard slicked his hair back with brylcreem and wore fake leopard skin, while Marc Bolan wore black eye make-up, feather boas and satin. This revival also affected aspects of mainstream interior decoration, including floor-coverings, with an advertisement for Nairn Cushion-floor from *House and Garden* September 1977 announcing 'Our floors say something about you.' On one side of the double-page spread is a Victorian revival bathroom with draped curtains, claw-footed bath with brass fittings and heavy, oak furniture. The copy for this image reads

Figure 48 Interior of Biba Store

'I'd like to have a maid to look after me.' Juxtaposed with this on the opposite page is a glamorous, 1930s revival bathroom adorned with the quote 'I wish I were a Hollywood film star' (p. 187). This bathroom features a sunken bath, a sweeping staircase with *moderne* handrail, a mirrored sink unit and rising sun mirrors (Figure 49). The range of revivalist styles on offer affords a characteristic example of post-modern plundering of the past.

The Designer Decade

By the 1980s the independent film-makers of Hollywood were dominant. The influence of Hollywood beyond the screen in the 'designer decade' was through the promotion of well-cut clothes and accessories. The bohemianism of the 1970s was superseded by the reassertion of the importance of the designer. In *Annie Hall* (1977) Diane Keaton plays the insecure female lead in well-cut but plain Ralph Lauren outfits. The transposition of male clothes to the female body, transmitted through the pages of *Vogue*, was immensely influential. It was simple enough to emulate the look by wearing second-hand men's jackets and jumpers and shirts with sleeves that drooped over your hands and had to be rolled back. Men's trousers in loose flannel with waistcoats could also be worn by women. As Bruzzi has argued: 'There was something paradoxically feminine about the Keaton-inspired fashion which pervaded every type of women's clothes shops in the late 1970s. By not being fitted and not accentuating the feminine curves the distance between the masculinity of the clothes and the femininity of the body became magnified ...' (1997: 177). The introduction of the yuppie, the powerful and ambitious individual who sought to fight her way to the top, became conflated with feminism and the adoption of male values and male dress by women in the 1980s. Diane Keaton in *Baby Boom* (1987) or Kelly McGillis in *Top Gun* (1986) exemplies the trend.

The male yuppie image was exploited by Michael Douglas in *Wall Street*. Richard Gere had played a sexy, male juvenile delinquent in *Looking for Mr Goodbar* (1977) opposite a nervous Diane Keaton. His black leather jacket, tight jeans and slobbish slouch made him at once a role model and an object of desire. His sexual magnetism on screen was again exploited in *American Gigolo* (1980), where he played Julian, a male prostitute and small-time designer. The film opens with Gere driving the ultimate yuppie vehicle, as perceived on the west coast of America, a BMW convertible. Blondie's feminist punk anthem, 'Call Me', blasts in the background as Gere drives with hair flowing in the

Figure 49 Cushionfloor Advertisement

wind and designer shades screening his eyes. The clothes Gere wears are a focal point of the film, as Stella Bruzzi has rightly observed (1997: 26). However, I wonder whether fans of Gere are really enjoying the clothes more than seeing Gere dance around the screen bare-chested, picking out matching Armani ties and shirts. Surely the thrill is in seeing him with as few clothes on as possible or tantalizingly half-naked? When I first saw the film in 1980 it spoke to me about the luxury and sexiness of designer clothes and interiors, but also about the emptiness of these possessions. In the height of yuppie consumerism the films seemed to be attacking materialism and ambition. The same goes for *Pretty Woman* (1990), where roles are reversed. This time Gere plays the client (Edward), albeit innocent, of a female hooker played by Julia Roberts: Gere is dressed by Cerruti 1881 in sharp suits to represent his wealthy businessman role – a role that needs to be cracked and revealed by Vivien. Commentators have deplored the materialism of the film and the way in which Vivien is transformed by Gere's cash and the clothes and lifestyle he offers her (Bruzzi 1997: 15). However, it should not be forgotten that Vivien rejects all this and leaves him to take up a place at college. Up and down Rodeo Drive the stupidity and snobbery of the sales staff are constantly highlighted, both when Gere takes Vivien back there armed with his gold credit card and when Vivien returns to a shop that had refused to serve her, laden with bags: she tells them that they have made a 'Big Mistake'. The portrayal of the apparent attraction, and simultaneous acknowledgement of the emptiness, of the yuppie lifestyle is a recurrent theme in 1980s Hollywood.

Conclusion

The most significant film of the 1990s in terms of box office takings has been the blockbuster, *Titanic* (1997). Made for a mind-boggling $200 million budget, the film still managed to clear a profit, much to the chagrin of the British popular press (Massey and Hammond 1999). Whilst the film enjoyed popularity because of its historical authenticity, or lack of it, and the amazing special effects, its main popularity in terms of post-modern glamour has been amongst teenage girls. It is the 9–18 age group that returned to see the film on average 2.5 times. This at first was due to the allure of teen idol Leonardo di Caprio. However, return visits were explained by the strength of the story and the female lead, Kate Winslett, as well as the Edwardian glamour of the clothing and décor recreated on screen. Following its release, the only perceivable influence beyond the screen was in terms of the hit song by Celine Dion staying at number one in the charts for twelve weeks in Britain and America. There were some alterations of hair style, with girls wearing their hair in a loose bun near the top of their head with playful tendrils deliberately being allowed to escape. By autumn 1998 the British high street retailers had had time to catch up with the popularity of the film, and shops such as *Top Shop* and *River Island* were selling beaded, high-waisted party dresses in layers of chiffon over satin. Dragonfly hair ornaments were available, as were delicate necklaces and bracelets. The fur-collared coat made a huge come-back, as did satin slippers and low-cut dresses. As has been the case throughout this book, this impact of Hollywood beyond the screen has been reviled by British cultural commentators, particularly in press reviews of the film and subsequent articles. The fact that it was teenage girls who constituted the largest audience for the film served to reinforce the prejudices of male commentators about the Americanization of British culture. From the time of the release of *Our Dancing Daughters* in Britain in 1929 right up until the release of *Titanic* in 1998 the British establishment's attitude has remained the same towards Hollywood cinema: it is vulgar, brash and far too influential for young women in particular to be exposed to.

As this book has demonstrated, the history of Hollywood beyond the screen is a history of individual fantasy and wish-fulfilment – of identity creation through high street fashion or customization. This important history of material culture and design has received scant attention to date, owing to the rigidity of disciplinary boundaries and deeply embedded cultural attitudes that this book has sought to expose and challenge. The most important aspect of the history presented in this book is that of a feminine, popular, glamorous style contrasted with a masculine, elitist, modernist style in architecture and design. The interplay between these two competing stylistic paradigms has formed the basis of this book, and their articulation is evident throughout the history of Hollywood beyond the screen.

Bibliography

Books

Abrams, M. (1959) *The Teenage Consumer*, London: London Press Exchange

Albrecht, D. (1986) *Designing Dreams: Modern Architecture in the Movies*, London: Thames and Hudson

Albrecht, D. (1997) *The Work of Charles and Ray Eames: A Legacy of Invention*, New York: Abrams

Appadurai, A. (ed.) (1986) *The Social Life of Things: Commodities in Cultural Perspective*, Cambridge: Cambridge University Press

Ash, J. and Wilson, E. (eds) (1992) *Chic Thrills: A Fashion Reader,* London: Harper Collins

Atwell, D. (1981) *Cathedrals of the Movies: A History of British Cinemas and Their Audiences*, London: The Architectural Press

Atwood, M. (1989) *Cat's Eye*, London: Bloomsbury

Balio, T. (ed.) (1990) *Hollywood in the Age of Television*, London: Unwin Hyman

Balio, T. (1993) *Grand Design: Hollywood as a Modern Business Enterprise, 1930–1939,* London: University of California Press

Barker, M. (1984) *A Haunt of Fears,* London: Pluto Press

Barker, N. (1989) *The Mezzanine*, Cambridge: Granta

Barr, C. (1977) *Ealing Studios,* London: Cameron & Taylor, David & Charles

Barr, C. (ed.) (1986) *All Our Yesterdays: 90 Years of British Cinema,* London: BFI

Basten, F. E. (1995) *Max Factor's Hollywood: Glamour, Movies, Make-Up*, Los Angeles: General Publishing Group

Bayer, P. (1992) *Art Deco Architecture: Design, Decoration and Detail from the Twenties and Thirties*, London: Thames & Hudson

Beaton, C. (1961) *The Wandering Years: Diaries 1922–1939*, London: Weidenfeld and Nicolson

Belton, J. (ed.) (1996) *Movies and Mass Culture*, London: Athlone

Berger, J. (1972) *Ways of Seeing*, London: BBC and Penguin Books

Bernstein, M. and Studlar, G. (eds) (1997) *Visions of the East: Orientalism in Film*, London: I. B. Tauris Publishers

Birmingham Museum and Art Gallery (1994) *BikeArt: The Art, Craft and Lifestyle of the Custom Bike Movement*, Birmingham: The Museum

Biskind, P. (1998) *Easy Riders, Raging Bulls*, London: Bloomsbury

Blumer, H. (1933) *Movies and Conduct*, New York: Macmillan

Bordwell, D., Staiger, J. and Thompson, K. (1988) *The Classical Hollywood Cinema: Film Style and Mode of Production to 1960*, London: Routledge

Boydell, C. (1996) *The Architect of Floors: Modernism, Art and Mario Dorn Designs*, Coggeshall: Schoeser

Breeze, C. (1993) *New York Deco*, New York: Rizzoli

Brode, D. (1992) *The Films of the Fifties*, New York: Carol Publishing

Bruzzi, S. (1997) *Undressing Cinema: Clothing and Identity in the Movies*, London: Routledge

Bryson, B. (1995) *Notes From a Small Island*, London: Black Swan

Buckley, C. and Walker, L. (n. d.) *Between the Wars: Architecture and Design on Tyneside 1919–1939*, Newcastle: Newcastle Polytechnic Gallery

Bush, D. J. (1975) *The Streamlined Decade*, New York: Brazillier

Calder, A. (1969) *The People's War: 1939–1945*, London: Pimlico

Campbell, C. (1987), *The Romantic Ethic and the Spirit of Modern Consumerism*, Oxford: Basil Blackwell

Capitman, B., Kinerk, M. D. and Wilhelm, D. W. (1994) *Rediscovering Art Deco U.S.A.: A Nationwide Tour of Architectural Delights*, New York: Viking Studio Books

Carter, E. (1937) *Seaside Houses and Bungalows*, London: Country Life

Caughie, J. (ed.) (1999) *Theories of Authorship*, London: Routledge

Chant, C. (ed.) (1989) *Science, Technology and Everyday Life 1870–1950*, London: Routledge/Open University

Cheney, S. and Cheney, M. C. (1936) *Art and the Machine*, New York: McGraw-Hill

Clark, C. E. (1986), *The American Family Home 1800–1960*, Chapel Hill NC: University of North Carolina Press

Constantino, M. (1997) *Men's Fashion in the Twentieth Century: From Frock Coats to Intelligent Fibres*, London: B. T. Batsford

Cook, P. (1996) *Fashioning the Nation: Costume and Identity and British Cinema*, London: BFI

Cook, P. and Dodd, P. (eds) (1993) *Women and Film: A Sight and Sound Reader*, London: BFI

Davies, K. (1983) *At Home in Manhattan: Modern Decorative Arts, 1925 to the Depression,* New Haven, CT: Yale University Art Gallery

Davies, R. L. (1993) *The Glamour Factory inside Hollywood's Big Studio System,* Dallas, TX: Southern Methodist University Press

Davis, M. L. (1996) *Bullocks Wilshire,* Los Angeles: Balcony Press

Dean, D. (1983) *The Thirties: Recalling the English Architectural Scene,* London: Trefoil

Decordova, R. (1990) *Picture Personalities: The Emergence of the Star System in America,* Urbana, IL: University of Illinois Press

Dickinson, M. and Street, S. (1985) *Cinema and The State: the British Film Industry and the British Government 1927–1984,* London: BFI

Dimbleby, D. and Reynolds, D. (1988) *An Ocean Apart: The Relationship Between Britain and America in the Twentieth Century,* London: Hodder & Stoughton

Doane, M. (1987) *The Desire to Desire: The Woman's Film of the 1940s,* London: Macmillan

Dyer, G. (1982) *Advertising as Communication,* London: Routledge

Dyer, R. (1997) *White,* London: Routledge

Dyson, P. (1996) *A Century of Cinema in Dorset 1896–1996,* Ferndown: Power Publications

Eidelberg, M. (ed.) (1991) *Design 1935–1965: What Modern Was,* New York: Harry N. Abrams

Ellery, D. (1994) *RMS Queen Mary: The World's Favourite Liner,* Blandford Forum: Waterfront Publications

Elsaesser, T. and Barker, A. (1990) *Early Cinema Space, Frame, Narrative,* London: BFI

Engelmeier, R. and Engelmeier, P. W. (eds) (1997) *Fashion in Film,* New York: Prestel

Farrand-Thorp, M. (1939) *America at the Movies,* New Haven, CT: Yale University Press

Forster, M. (1995*) Hidden Lives: A Family Memoir,* London: Penguin Books

Forsyth, A. (1987) *Art and Design on the Greatest British Liners,* Exhibition Catalogue, Southampton: Southampton City Art Gallery

Forty, A. (1986) *Objects of Desire,* London: Thames & Hudson

Foster, H. (1993) *Compulsive Beauty,* Cambridge, MA: MIT Press

Franci, G., Mangaroni, R. and Zago, E. (1997) *A Journey Through American Art Deco,* Seattle: University of Washington Press

Frankl, P. T. (1972) *Form and Re-Form,* New York: Hacker Art Books (First published, 1930.)

Freud, S. (1984) *On Metapsychology: The Theory of Psychoanalysis,* Harmondsworth: Penguin

Frisby, D. and Featherstone, M. (eds) (1997) *Simmel On Culture*, London: Sage

Fry, S. (1998) *Moab Is My Washpot*, London: Arrow

Gaines, J. and Herzog, C. (eds) (1990) *Fabrications: Costume and the Female Body*, London: Routledge

Garner, P. and Mellor, D. A. (1994) *Cecil Beaton*, London: Jonathan Cape

Gebhard, D. (1996) *The National Trust Guide to Art Deco in America*, Washington DC: John Wiley & Sons

Gebhard, D. and Von Breton, H. (1969) *H. Kem Weber: The Moderne in Southern California, 1920 through 1941*, Santa Barbara CA: The Art Galleries, University of California

Gent, J. B. (1992) *Croydon Between the Wars: Photographs From The Period 1919 to 1939*, South Croydon: Croydon Natural History and Scientific Society Ltd

Gilroy, P. (1993) *The Black Atlantic: Modernity and Double Consciousness*, London: Verso

Gledhill, C. (ed.) (1991) *Stardom: Industry of Desire*, London: Routledge

Gledhill, C. and Swanson, G. (eds) (1996) *Nationalising Femininity: Culture, Sexuality and British Cinema in the Second World War*, Manchester: Manchester University Press

Gray, R. (1996) *Cinemas in Britain: One Hundred Years of Cinema Architecture*, London: Lund Humphries

Greif, M. (1975) *Depression Modern: The Thirties Style in America*, London: Universe Press

Gronberg, T. (1998) *Designs, Modernity 1920's*, Manchester: Manchester University Press

Gropius, W. (1936), *The New Architecture and the Bauhaus*, trans. Morton Shand, London: Faber & Faber

Guilbaut, S. (1984) *How New York Stole the Idea of Modern Art: Abstract Expressionism, Freedom and Cold War*, Chicago: University of Chicago Press

Hall, S. (ed.) (1997) *Representation: Cultural Representations and Signifying Practices*, London: Sage

Hall, S. and Jefferson, T. (eds) (1993) *Resistance Through Rituals: Youth Subcultures in Post-War Britain*, London: Routledge

Hall, S., Held, D. and McGrew, T. (eds) (1992) *Modernity and its Futures*, Cambridge: Polity Press/Open University

Harding, C. and Lewis, B. (eds) (1993) *The Popular Experience of Cinema*, Bradford: National Museum of Photography Film/TV

Hardy, D. and Ward, C. (1986) *Goodnight Campers,* London: Mansell Publishing

Hardy, P. (1986) *The Encyclopaedia of Science Fiction Movies*, London: Octopus Books

Harper, S. (1994) *Picturing the Past: The Rise and Fall of the British Costume Film*, London: BFI

Hatchard, D. (1990) *Southampton/Eastleigh Airport*, Southampton: Kingfisher Publications

Heide, R. and Gilman, J. (1991) *Popular Art Deco: Depression Era Style and Design*, London: Abbeville Press

Heisner, B. (1990) *Hollywood Art: Art Direction in the Days of the Great Studios*, London: St James Press

Hillier, B. (1997) *Art Deco Style*, London: Phaidon

Hoggart, R. (1958) *The Uses of Literacy: Aspects of Working-class Life with Special Reference to Publications and Entertainments*, Harmondsworth: Penguin

Hooks, B. (1996) *Reel to Real: Race, Sex and Class at the Movies*, London: Routledge

Huyssen, A. (1986) *After The Great Divide: Modernism, Mass Culture, Post-Modernism*, Basingstoke: Macmillan

Ionides, B. (1926) *Colour and Interior Decoration*, London: Country Life

Ionides, B. (1934) *Colour in Everyday Rooms: With Remarks on Sundry Aspects of Decoration*, London: Country Life

Jacobs, L. (1995) *The Wages of Sin: Censorship and the Fallen Woman Film, 1928–1942*, London: University of California Press

Jahn, M. (1973) *Rock: From Elvis Presley to the Rolling Stones*, New York: Quadrangle/New York Times Book Co.

Jarvie, I. (1992) *Hollywood's Overseas Campaign: The North Atlantic Movie Trade, 1920–1950*, Cambridge: Cambridge University Press

Joel, D. (1969) *Furniture Design Set Free: The British Furniture Revolution from 1851 to the Present Day*, London: J. M. Dent

Johnson, P. and Hitchcocks, H. R. (1996) *The International Style*, New York: Norton

King, A. (1995) *The Bungalow*, Oxford: Oxford University Press

Kingery, W. D. (1996) *Learning From Things: Method and Theory of Material Culture Studies*, Washington and London: Smithsonian Institution Press

Kirkham, P. (1995) *Charles and Ray Eames: Designers of the Twentieth Century*, London: MIT Press

Kirkham, P. and Attfield, J. (eds) (1996) *The Gendered Object*, Manchester and New York: Manchester University Press

Kwint, M., Breward, C. and Aynsley, J. (eds) (1999) *Material Memories: Design and Evocation*, Oxford: Berg

Lant, A. (1991) *Blackout: Reinventing Women for Wartime British Cinema,* Princeton, NJ: Princeton University Press

Laver, J. (1969) *Fashion,* London: Thames & Hudson

Leese, E. (1991) *Costume Design in the Movies,* New York: Dover Publications

Leiss, W.K. and Jhally, S. (1986) *Social Communication in Advertising,* London: Methuen

Lindley, K . (1973) *Seaside Architecture,* London: Hugh Evelyn

Lott, T. (1996) *The Scent of Dried Roses,* London: Viking

Lubar, S. and Kingery, W. D. (1993*) History From Things: Essays on Material Culture,* Washington and London: Smithsonian Institution Press

Lyons, D. and Weinberg, A.D. (eds) (1995) *Edward Hopper and the American Imagination,* London: Whitney Museum of American Art in Association with W. W. Norton and Company, New York

MacCarthy, F. (1979) *A History of British Design* (2nd Edition), London: George Allen & Unwin Ltd

McRobbie, A. (1994) *Postmodernism and Popular Culture,* London: Routledge

McRobbie, A. and Nava, M. (eds) (1991) *Gender and Generation,* London: Macmillan Educational

Mandelbaum, H. and Myers, E. (1985) *Screen Deco: A Celebration of High Style in Hollywood,* Bromley: Columbus Books.

Marchand, R. (1985) *Advertising the American Dream: Making Way for Modernity,* Berkeley, CA: University of California Press

Massey, A. (1990*) Interior Design of the Twentieth Century,* London: Thames & Hudson

Massey, A. (1995) *The Independent Group: Modernism and Mass Culture in Britain 1945–59,* Manchester: Manchester University Press

Massey, A. (ed.) (1997) *Romancing Hollywood: The Construction and Reception of Glamour,* Southampton: Millais Gallery

Mayer, J. P. (1948) *British Cinemas and Their Audiences,* London: Dennis Dobson

Meikle, J. (1979) *Twentieth-Century Limited: Industrial Design in America 1925–1939,* Philadelphia: Temple University Press

Miller, D. (1987) *Material Culture and Mass Consumption,* Oxford: Blackwell

Miller, D. (ed.) (1995) *Acknowledging Consumption: A Review of New Studies,* London: Routledge

Miller, D. (ed.) (1996) *Material Cultures: Why Some Things Matter,* London: UCL Press

Miller, T. (1997) *The Avengers,* London: BFI

Mirzoeff, N. (ed.) (1998) *The Visual Culture Reader,* London: Routledge

Mirzoeff, N. (1999) *An Introduction to Visual Culture,* London: Routledge

Morgan, J. (1991) *Edwina Mountbatten: A Life of Her Own,* London: Harper Collins

Murphy, R. (ed.) (1997) *The British Cinema Book,* London: BFI

Myerscough-Walker, R. (1940) *Stage and Film Décor,* London: Pitman

Oliver, P. , Davis, I. and Bentley, I. (1994) *Dunroamin': The Suburban Semi and Its Enemies,* London: Pimlico

Patmore, D. (1933) *Colour Schemes for the Modern Home,* London: The Studio Limited

Peiss, K. (1986) *Cheap Amusements: Working Women and Leisure in Turn-of-the-Century New York,* Philadelphia: Temple University Press

Pevsner, N. (1937) *An Enquiry into Industrial Art in England,* Cambridge: Cambridge University Press

Pevsner, N. and Newman, J. (1972) *The Buildings of England*: *Dorset,* Harmondsworth: Penguin

Powers, A. (1989) *Oliver Hill: Architect and Lover of Life 1887–1968,* London: Mouton Publications

Priestley, J. B. (1987) *An English Journey: being a rambling but truthful account of what one man saw ... during the Autumn of the year 1933,* London: Heinemann & Gollancz (First Published 1934.)

Read, S. (1986) *Hello Campers! Celebrating 50 Years of Butlins,* London: Bantam

Redhead, S. (1997) *Post-Fandom and the Millennial Blues,* London: Routledge

Richards, J. (1984) *The Age of the Dream Palace: Cinema and Society in Britain 1930–39,* London: Routledge & Kegan Paul

Rolf-Renner, G. (1993) *Edward Hopper 1882–1967: Transformation of the Real,* London: Benedikt Taschen

Rosenberg, E. (1992) *Spreading the American Dream,* New York: Hill and Wang

The Royal Birkdale Club (1998) *The Royal Birkdale Golf Club in the Year of its Eighth Open Championship,* Liverpool: Programme Publications

Schlereth, T. J. (ed.) (1982) *Material Culture Studies in America,* Nashville, TN: American Association for State and Local History

Schlereth, T. J. (1990) *Cultural History and Material Culture: Everyday Life, Landscapes, Museums,* Charlottesville, VA and London: University Press of Virginia

Sembach, K. J. (1972) *Into the Thirties: Style and Design 1927–1934,* London: Thames & Hudson

Sharp, D. (1969) *Picture Palaces and Other Buildings for the Movies*, London: Evelyn

Short, K. R. M. (ed.) (1983) *Film and Radio Propaganda in World War 2*, London: Croom Helm

Skeggs, B. (ed.) (1995) *Feminist Cultural Theory: Process and Production*, Manchester: Manchester University Press

Sklar, R. (1994) *Movie-Made America: A Cultural History of American Movies*, New York: Vintage Books

Smith, T. (1993) *Making the Modern: Industry, Art, and Design in America*, Chicago and London: The University of Chicago Press

Smithells, R. (1939) *Country Life Book of Small Houses*, London: Country Life

Sothebys (1987) *The Contents of Wilsford Manor*, London: Sothebys

Sparke, P. (1995) *As Long as It's Pink: The Sexual Politics of Taste*, London: Pandora

Sparke, P. , Hodges, F., Dent Coad, E. and Stone, A. (1986) *Design Source Book : A Visual Reference to Design from 1850 to the Present Day*, London: Macdonald Orbis

Stansfield, C. (1986) *Beside The Seaside*, Preston: The Thirties Society

Stead, P. (1989) *Film and The Working Class: The Feature Film in British and American Society*, London: Routledge

Steedman, C. (1986) *Landscape for a Good Woman*, London: Virago

Steele, J. (1995) *Queen Mary*, London: Phaidon

Steele, J. (1998) *Pierre Koenig*, London: Phaidon

Stones, B. (1993) *America Goes to the Movies: 100 Years of Motion Picture Exhibition*, North Hollywood: National Association of Theatre Owners

Street, S. (1997) *British National Cinema*, London: Routledge

Strinati, D. and Wagg, S. (1992) *Come on Down?: Popular Media Culture in Post-War Britain*, London: Routledge

Studlar, G. (1996) *This Mad Masquerade: Stardom and Masculinity in the Jazz Age*, New York: Columbia University Press

Swann, P. (1987) *The Hollywood Feature Film in Post-War Britain*, Beckenham: Croom Helm

Symons, J. (1975) *The Thirties: A Dream Revolved*, London: Faber

Tapert, A. (1998) *The Power of Glamour: The Women Who Defined the Magic of Stardom*, London: Aurum Press

Thompson, E. P. (1963) *The Making of the English Working Class*, London: Gollancz

Vasey, R. (1997) *The World According to Hollywood: 1918–1939*, Exeter: University of Exeter Press

Ward, C. (1986) *Goodnight Campers: The History of the British Holiday Camp*, London: Mansell

Watts, S. (ed.) (1938) *Behind The Screen: How Films Are Made*, London: Arthur Baker

Waugh, E. (1988) *A Handful of Dust*, London: Penguin (First published 1934.)

Weedon, C. (1997) *Feminist Practice and Poststructuralist Theory*, Oxford: Blackwell

Wharton, E. and Codman Jr, O. (1987) *The Decoration of Houses*, New York: Norton (First published 1902.)

Wiener, M. J. (1992) *English Culture and the Decline of the Industrial Spirit 1850–1980*, Harmondsworth: Penguin

Williams, R. (1983) *Culture and Society 1780–1950*, New York: Columbia University Press (First published 1958.)

Wilson, R. G., Pilgrim, D. H. and Tashjian, D. (1986) *The Machine Age in America, 1918–1941*, New York: Harry N. Abrams

Wolfe, T. (1968) *The Kandy-Kolored Tangerine-Flake Streamline Baby*, London: Mayflower (First published 1965.)

York Oral History Project (1988) *York Memories of Stage and Screen: Personal Accounts of York's Theatres and Cinemas 1900–1960*, York: York Oral History Project

Zukowsky, J. (1996) *Building for Air Travel: Architecture and Design for Commercial Aviation*, Prestel: London.

Articles

Allen, J. (1980) 'The Film Viewer as Consumer', *Quarterly Review of Film Studies*, Vol. 5, Fall, pp. 481–99

Alloway, L. (1958) 'The Arts and the Mass Media', *Architectural Design*, No. 28, February, pp. 84–5

Alloway, L. (1961) 'Architecture and the Modern Cinema', *The Listener*, Vol. LXV, No. 1682, 22 June, pp. 1085–6

Alloway, L. (1963) 'The Iconography of the Movies', *Movie*, Febuary/March, pp. 7–9

Bailey-Cutts, A. (1938) 'Homes of Tomorrow in the Movies of Today', *California Arts & Architecture*, Vol. 54, November

Barr, A. (1966) 'Preface', in H.-R. Hitchcock and P. Johnson (eds), *The International Style* (New York: Norton), pp. 11–16

Bennett, T. (1982) 'Text and Social Process: the Case of James Bond', *Screen Education*, Vol. 10 (41), pp. 3–14

Betjeman, J. (1930) '1830–1930–Still Going Strong: A Guide to the Recent History of Interior Decoration', *Architectural Review,* May, pp. 231–41

Bicat, A. (1970) 'Fifties Children: Sixties People', in V. Bogdanor and R. Skidelsky (eds), *The Age of Affluence, 1951–1964,* London: Macmillan

Binney, M. (1997) 'Staying Power', *The Times Magazine,* 20 December, pp. 14–21

Birtwistle, W. (1934) 'Bournemouth as a Holiday Resort', in Dr S Watson-Smith, *The Book of Bournemouth: Written for the 102 Annual Meeting of the British Medical Association – Bournemouth July 1934,* Bournemouth: Messrs. Pardy & Son, pp. 55–6

Borhek, J. T. (1989) 'Rods, Choppers and Restorations: The Modifications and Re-Creation of Production Motor Vehicles in America', *Journal of Popular Culture,* Vol. 22 (4), Spring, pp. 97–108

Boumphrey, G. (1935) 'Betty Joel', *Architectural Review,* November, pp. 205–6

Boumphrey, G. (1936) 'Mr. Boumphrey's Reply', *Architectural Review,* January, p. 50

Browning, H. E. and Sorrell, A. A. (1954) 'Cinemas and Cinema-Going in Great Britain', *Journal of the Royal Statistical Society ,* Series A, Part 2

Brunsdon, C. (1991) 'Pedagogies of the Feminine: Feminist Reading and Women's Genres', *Screen,* 32:4 Winter, pp. 364–81

Buckley, C. (1998) 'On The Margins: Theorizing The History and Significance of Making and Designing Clothes at Home', *Journal of Design History,* No. 2, pp. 157–71

Campbell, C. (1998) 'Consumption and the Rhetorics of Need and Want', *Journal of Design History,* Vol. 11, No. 3, pp. 235–46

Campbell, L. (1996) 'Patterns of the Modern House', *Twentieth Century Society: Architecture 2,* pp. 41–50

Carrick, E. (1930) 'Moving Picture Sets: A Medium for the Architect', *Architectural Record,* Vol. 67, May, pp. 440–4

Carroll, C. (1935) 'Art Direction For Films', *Design For To-Day,* October, pp. 391–5

Deskey, D. (1933) 'The Rise of American Architecture and Design', *The Studio,* Vol. 105, 1933, pp. 260–73

Eckert, C. (1978) 'The Carole Lombard in Macy's Window', *Quarterly Review of Film Studies,* Vol. 3, No. 1, Winter 1978, pp. 1–21

Elms, R. (1986) 'Ditching the Drabbies: A Style for Socialism', *New Socialist,* No. 38, May, pp. 12–15

Erengis, G. P. (1965) 'Cedric Gibbons: Set A Standard for Art Direction That Raised The Movies' Cultural Level', *Films in Review,* April, pp. 217–32

Eustis, M. (1937) 'Designing for the Movies: Gibbons of MGM', *Theatre Arts Monthly,* October, pp. 783–98

Eyles, A. (1997) 'Exhibition and the Cinema Going Experience', in R. Murphy (ed.), *The British Cinema Book,* pp. 217–25, London: BFI

Gaines, J. (1989) 'The Queen Christina Tie-Ups: Convergence of Show Window and Screen', *Quarterly Review of Film and Video,* Vol. 11, pp. 35–60

Gebhard, D. (1970) 'The Moderne in the US', *Architectural Association Quarterly,* July, pp. 4–19

Geraghty, C. (1997) 'Women and Sixties British Cinema: The Development of the "Darling" girl', in R. Murphy (ed.), *The British Cinema Book,* pp. 154–66, London:BFI

Geran, M. (1980) 'Women in Design', *Interior Design,* Vol. 51, No. 2, February, pp. 257–67

Glancy, J. (1998) 'Home of the Steel Ideal', *The Guardian Weekend,* 7 November, pp. 80–4

Godden, R. (1998) 'Introduction' to F. S. Fitzgerald, *Tender is the Night,* London: Penguin Books

Gould, J. (1996) 'Gazetteer of Modern Houses in the United Kingdom and the Republic of Ireland', in *Twentieth Century Architecture 2,* pp. 111–28, London: The 20th Century Society

Grigson, G. (1935) 'Design of the Temporary Home', *The Studio,* Vol. CX, No. 511, October 1935, pp. 191–201

Hadley, C. (1998) 'The Last Fire', *The Guardian Weekend,* 4 July, pp. 30–4

Harper, S. and Porter, V. (1999) 'Cinema Audience Tastes in 1950s Britain', *Journal of Popular British Cinema,* Vol. 2, pp. 66–82

Hayward, S. (1998) 'Good Design is Largely a Matter of Common Sense: Questioning the Meaning and Ownership of a Twentieth-Century Orthodoxy', *Journal of Design History,* 11, pp. 217–33

Hebdige, D. (1981a) 'Toward a Cartography of Taste 1935–1962', *Block* 4, pp. 39–56

Hebdige, D. (1981b) 'Object as Image: The Italian Scooter Cycle', *Block* 5, pp. 44–64

Heller, S. (1995) 'Commercial Modernism: American Design Style 1925–1933', *Print,* Vol. 49, No. 5, Sept.–Oct., pp. 58–68, 122

Hiley, N. (1999) 'Let's Go to the Pictures: The British Cinema Audience in the 1920s and 1930s', *Journal of Popular British Cinema,* Vol. 2, pp. 39–53

Hitchcock, H.-R. (1928) 'Some American Interiors in the Modern Style', *Architectural Record*, Vol. 64, September, pp. 235–44

'Home Talent' (1939) *House Beautiful*, January, pp. 18–19

Jacobowitz, F. and Lippe, R. (1992) 'Empowering Glamour', *Cineaction*, Vol. 26/27, Winter 1992, pp. 2–11

Joel, B. (1935) 'A House and a Home', in J. de la Valette (ed.), *The Conquest of Ugliness: A Collection of Contemporary Views on the Place of Art in Industry*, pp. 87–97, London: Methuen

Joel, B. (1936) ''Correspondence', *Architectural Review*, January, p. 49

Kirkham, P. (1995) 'Dress, Dance, Dreams, and Fashion and Fantasy in Dance Halls', *Journal of Design History*, Vol. 8, No. 3, pp. 195–214

Lacey, J. (1999) 'Seeing Through Happiness: Hollywood Musicals and the Construction of the American Dream in Liverpool in the 1950s', *Journal of Popular British Cinema*, Vol. 2, pp. 54–65

Lachenbruch, J. (1921) 'Interior Decoration for the Movies: Studies from the Work of Cedric Gibbons and Gilbert White', *Arts and Decoration*, January, pp. 201 and 205

Macaulay, S. (1999) 'Hollywood's Hot Summer', *The Times*, 6 September, p. 45

McNeil, P. (1994) 'Designing Women: Gender, Sexuality and the Interior Decorator, *c*.1890–1940', *Art History*, Vol. 17, No. 4, December 1994, pp. 631–57

Mambrino, A. (1927) 'Reflections on Atmosphere: The Modern London Hotel', *Architectural Review*, Vol 61, April, pp. 129–37

Massey, A. (1993) 'Biba: Interior Lifestyles', in Laing Art Gallery, *Biba: The Label, The Look, The Lifestyle*, Newcastle: Tyne and Wear Museums, pp. 20–5

Massey, A. and Hammond, M. (1999) 'It Was True! How Can you Laugh!?', in *Titanic: An Anatomy of a Blockbuster*, New Brunswick, NJ: Rutgers University Press, pp. 239–64

Miller, D. (1984) 'Modernism and Suburbia as Material Ideology', in D. Miller and C. Tilley (eds), *Ideology, Power and Prehistory*, Cambridge: Cambridge University Press

Moat, J. (1999) 'Resources on Film Exhibition and Reception at the BFI National Library', *Journal of Popular British Cinema*, No. 2, pp. 132–5

Modleski, T. (1986) 'Femininity as Mas(k)querade: A Feminist Approach to Mass Culture', in C. MacCabe (ed.), *High Theory/Low Culture*, Manchester: Manchester University Press

Mulvey, L. (1975) 'Visual Pleasure and Narrative Cinema', *Screen*, Vol. 16, No. 3, Autumn, pp. 6–18

Partington, A. (1985) 'Design Knowledge and Feminism', *Feminist Arts News*, Vol. 2, No. 3, December, pp. 9–13

Powers, A. (1986) 'Traveling in Style", review of *Art on the Liners*, *The Spectator*, 31 May

Pumphrey, M. (1987) 'The Flapper, The Housewife and the Making of Modernity', *Cultural Studies*, No. 1, Vol. 2, May 1987, pp. 179–94

Reilly, P. (1967) 'The Challenge of Pop', *Architectural Review*, Vol. 142, pp. 255–7

Rowson, S. (1936) 'A Statistical Survey of the Cinema Industry in Great Britain in 1934', *Journal of the Royal Statistical Society*, Vol. 99

Shand, P. Morton (1931) 'Say it in Spanish: The Latest Phase in Kinema Decoration', *The Ideal Kinema*, Vol. 171, No. 1256, May 14, pp. 4 and 15

Skinner, J. (1994) 'The Firestone Factory 1928–1980', *The Journal of the Twentieth Century Society*, No 1, Summer, pp. 11–22

Smithson, A. and Smithson, P. (1966) 'Eames Collection', *Architectural Design*, September, pp. 432–71

Stacey, J. (1994) 'Hollywood Memories', *Screen*, Vol. 35 (4), Winter, pp. 317–35

Stead, P. (1981) 'Hollywood's Message for the World: The British Response in the 1930s', *Historical Journal of Film, Radio and Television*, Vol. 1, pp. 18–32

Thumin, J. (1996) 'Film and Female Identity: Questions of Method in Investigating Representations of Women in Popular Culture', in C. MacCabe and D. Petrie (eds), *New Scholarship from BFI Research*, London: BFI

Walkerdine, V. (1991) 'Behind the Painted Smile', in *Family Snaps: The Meaning of Domestic Photography*, ed. J. Spence and P. Holland, London: Virago

Webb, M. (1990) 'Cedric Gibbons and The MGM Style: The Pioneering Art Director Who Brought Modernism to the Movies', *Architectural Digest*, April, pp. 103, 104, 108, 112

Wilk, C. (1995) 'Who Was Betty Joel?: British Furniture Design Between the Wars', *Apollo*, Vol. CXLII, No. 41, June, pp. 7–11

Wilson, E. (1993) 'Audrey Hepburn: Fashion, Film and the 50s', in P. Cook and P. Dodd, *Women and Film: A Sight and Sound Reader*, BFI: London

Unpublished

BFI, Pressbooks for *Our Dancing Daughters*, *Our Blushing Brides* and *Our Modern Maidens*

Interviews (1998) by author with Gwen Carr and Harry Massey

Kuhn, A. (1997a) *Cinema Culture in 1930s Britain: End of Award Report*

Kuhn, A. (1997b) *Cinemagoing in the 1930s: Report of a Questionnaire Survey*

Paynton, V. C. (1995) 'The "Ideal Kinema": Class, Gender and Cinema Design', M.Phil. Thesis, Southampton Institute.

Material collected for *Fathers of Pop* (1979), an Arts Council film, but largely unused:

Transcripts of interviews by Reyner Banham of: Lawrence Alloway (25 May 1977); Frank Cordell, Richard Hamilton, Nigel Henderson, Dorothy Morland, Richard Smith, Peter and Alison Smithson, Will Turnbull (all undated)

Transcript of discussion between: Mary and Reyner Banham, John McHale, Magda Cordell dated 30 May 1977; Toni del Renzio, Reyner Banham and Richard Hamilton (undated)

Index